Guest of the Fuhrer

By Les Shorrock

A true account of a prisoner of war from 1940 until 1945

With an introduction by Lee Jackson

Printed in the United Kingdom

First Printed, August 2017

Second Edition, October 2017

Cover Illustration – Dave Morris

Dtmphotography.co.uk

Acknowledge

Preparing my Grandads book for
could not have achieved without
and family including:

Shaun Cullen who advised me, assisted me with the editing
and layout of the book.

Vince Prati who advised me on the transforming of the book
from the original manuscript.

Dave Morris who gave up his own time to help me design the
front cover of the book.

Margaret Alderson for supplying me with pictures of her
Father, Harry Alderson.

Contents

Introduction

My earliest memories of my Grandad were of an honest, proud, respectable, upstanding man who used to always take me as a young child to the local parks in south east London. He always enjoyed the outdoors. He was a man that always had time for me and my two siblings, Stacey and Tiffany.

My Grandad was such an intelligent man, even though he left school at 14 years of age. He always knew the answer to any question I had.

He married my Grandmother, Gladys in 1947 and had one child, my Mother, Pauline. My Grandad was a hard worker, working in the city most of his life in various office jobs. Once he retired, he would spend the day walking around the local parks and taking time out to spend with me, especially every Saturday when we would take a bus ride out into the countryside of Kent.

He always used to tell me stories from World War II, I always sat there, fascinated by his tales of daring and adventure as a reluctant 'Guest of the Fuhrer'.

He loved tv shows such as Dad's Army, It Ain't Half Hot Mum and The Phil Silvers show. He self-taught himself to play the guitar, and used to play along to tapes of his favourite singers, Bing Crosby and Al Jolson.

He wrote this book in 1980 as an attempt to preserve his memories for myself and future generations to come.

Unlike some other World War II prisoner accounts, my Grandad had no problem in putting his memories onto paper.

My Grandad was a role model for me.

To my great loss, he passed away in 1991 aged 71, but I still hold dear, many memories of him and the times he spent with me.

This book is dedicated to all people who have been a prisoner in any war in the world.

In 1939, I was eighteen years of age and just over six feet tall. I lived with my family on an estate in Lewisham, south east London.

My Father was a wonderful man, very tall, well educated, in fact a Christian Gentleman. He was employed in the architect's department of the London County Council, as it then was, at a branch in Rye Lane, Peckham. He had served in the 1914–18 war, in which his two brothers also fought, George Shorrock, a Captain[1] in the R.AM.C[2] and his younger brother, Lieut Ralph Dudley Shorrock, Royal Fusiliers, killed at Vimy Ridge in 1917, aged 20. Ralph who was killed before I was born, in 1920, was a gifted pianist and composer, whose death affected my father very deeply.[3]

My Father, who was slightly gassed, survived the war without being wounded, but now in early 1939 was to die on 6th March, aged 50, from the illness I am sure must have been at least partly caused by the effect, on his health, of those terrible war years in the trenches.

My mother lost her only brother, aged 18 years, killed at Zeebrugge.[4]

[1] *George Shorrock was actually listed in records as a staff sergeant, not a Captain.*

[2] *Royal Army Medical Corps.*

[3] *Ralph Dudley Shorrock's correct name was actually Thomas Dudley Ralph Shorrock and he died on 20th September 1917 at the battle of The Menin Road Ridge. He was listed in army records as a temporary 2nd Lieutenant.*

[4] *Her brother was called Herbert Bryan. Army records show that he was killed on 21st July 1915 in Flanders, France at the age of 17.*

I also had an older brother, an older sister, and two younger sisters, and we were a happy family despite the tragedy in 1931, when after the birth of my younger sister, my mother suffered a long illness, which left her crippled for the rest of her 47 years of life.

In those pre-war days of 1939, although there were over a million people unemployed, and life was very hard, yet my generation were far kinder and compassionate than they appear to be today.[5] We were always taught to respect girls, to give up our seat on public vehicles, and I'm sure we lived in a more Christian attitude towards life, probably due to the influence of our parents, our teachers, and the Sunday schools we attended, and of course the boy's clubs, one of the conditions of membership being that we attended church each Sunday. Naturally like other lads of my age, we would try to attend as infrequently as possible, consequently often being expelled from the clubs, either for that or our failure to afford the regular subscription of three pence or sixpence per week required. We were always reinstated however, on our apologies, and well-meant promises to improve.

We enjoyed ourselves. Besides the rough games of cricket and football, cycling, which was one of the cheapest and most popular past times, we also had the cinema, where for sixpence or nine pence we could spend hours seeing musicals, or black and white films of Hollywood giants of the screen. We realised later in life, these "giants" were almost all tired little men, in baggy trousers, often wearing built – up shoes to make them appear taller, and incessantly smoking cigarettes.

[5] *1980*

Of all the movie world razzamatazz, and glitter, nearly everyone appreciated Bing Crosby, who was the greatest talented crooner of our time. We always enjoyed his films; we tried to imitate him, although alas we were unable to afford the money to purchase the gramophone records, as they were then called.

I was employed in 1939, in an export merchant office in Basinghall Street, near the Bank of England. This company was an agency that shipped goods of almost every kind to the South African market and their principal branches were at Johannesburg, Port Elizabeth, Cape Town, East London and other places. They were good employers and I had been with them since March 1937, employed in a junior capacity in which one had to serve in order to obtain promotion in the future. The hours were marvellous, 9.30am – 5.00pm which was exceptional for those times and the partners of the company must have been tolerant people for they gave us latitude and I remember clearly the practical jokes and good humour that abounded.

My friend who worked next to me, Vic Mason, lived in East Ham and would cycle over to see me occasionally on a summer evening. Vic was my age and had been a boy scout. He was a clean living, well-built lad, keen on sport and keeping fit. Moreover, he was a non – smoker and I regret that at that time, I used to smoke five cigarettes a day, which was all I could afford. In those days, nearly everyone I knew smoked cigarettes or a pipe. It was considered the manly thing to do and I am afraid such an attitude was considerably promoted and advertised prominently. Vic urged me to give up smoking and suggested that he took my cigarettes away and lock them up in his desk drawer, which he did. He would then refuse to give me one, although I used to plead with him. With laughter on his face, he would suggest I get on the floor and kneel in supplication, which I did, laughing myself. He would then give me one and I would then have to go through another hilarious performance to obtain another. I am glad to say that I have been a non – smoker now for over thirty years.

I used to earn a weekly wage of almost £2, which was quite a fair salary in those days as a junior. I used to give my mother as much as possible, especially after the death of my father for only my brother, older sister and I, were able to work. I left enough to be able to afford a visit once a week to the cinema and to enable me to purchase the small supply of cigarettes. One Friday, after being paid in the morning, I visited a sandwich shop, to buy a sandwich for lunch, but on returning to the office I discovered to my horror that I had just lost a pound note. This was a terrible catastrophe, as it meant everything to me to be able to pay my mother. I told Vic what had happened and he advised me to return to the sandwich shop, which I did. They asked me to call back before they closed at 5pm to see if anyone had handed in the note. I could not believe I could be so lucky, and confided my anxiety to Vic. He immediately went along the passageway to another office and quickly returned, pressing a pound note in my hand. He had drawn all his savings from a club run by the company. I gasped out my thanks and appreciation for this wonderful gesture, but I could see no hope of being able to repay him. He told me not to worry but try to pay him three pence a week. I was tremendously grateful and at 5pm I returned to the shop where to my utter joy they handed me my pound note which had been handed in by some honest customer. I thanked them, and rushed back in time to catch Vic, before he left for home to return his £1. I never forgot this unselfish act, for in the hardship of those days, only those who went through them would appreciate what it meant to me.

The war clouds were gathering, and the two comedians, Hitler and Mussolini, were ranting and raving, Il Duce, for the return of Tunis, Corsica and Nice, the Fuhrer, for Lebensraum, and everything else that suited him. Austria, Sudetenland, Czechoslovakia, had been annexed and soon it was to be the turn of Poland.

Vic had already enlisted in the Territorial Army at a local Anti-Aircraft regiment. He had repeatedly asked me to join his unit but I had hesitated, mainly because of the distance of travel three times a week, from Lewisham to East Ham, the cost of that journey, and the time involved, at the end of a working day. Despite this, I finally decided to enlist at his depot and broke the news to him one early morning in April 1939. Vic beamed at me when I told him and replied "Too late Sharkey, we're full up". His pet name for me was Sharkey, because my name was Shorrock. I was disappointed at his news, but nevertheless decided to enlist somewhere, imagining to myself the consternation in Rome and Berlin, when the information reached them of their ultimate downfall! One of my pals, in the street where I lived, also was keen to enlist, so together we set out one evening to try our luck.

We approached a local AA unit (Anti – Aircraft), stationed at Baring Road, Grove Park, only to be informed that they were also fully situated. We next tried the 91st Field Regiment R.A.

(TA) the Headquarters of which was at Ennersdale Road, Lewisham, a short distance from where we lived. We were accepted, sworn in, signed, received the King's shilling each and now became, as the term was, Saturday night soldiers, namely Gunner Jack Richards. Army No. 892704 and Gunner Leslie Shorrock 892705. From then on, we paraded at Ennersdale Road, two or three times a week, to be instructed in the art of manipulating 4.5 Howitzers, or to drive impressed motor vehicles, or any other useful tasks, which could be found to match our enthusiasm.

Besides being issued with ancient ill-fitting uniforms and equipment, we also received a silver badge marked TA, to be worn on our civilian clothes and sold at 2/6d, or 15 pence to-day. We signed for these badges and I still have the slip of paper marked April 1939, warning us of the cost of losing this item. So, each week we reported to the drill hall, where we found many of our school friends and joined them in trundling and man-handling these pieces of artillery together with the intricate equipment, dummy shells, etc, in order to instil some knowledge of how to use these. After drill nights were finished most of the lads retired to the canteen, where refreshment of beer was always readily available, but as I was and still am a tea-totaller, I rarely took part in these festive occasions.

Upon joining the T.A. my employers expressed their appreciation and informed me that I was now entitled to an extra fortnight's holiday, to compensate for the two weeks I would spend at the army camp each year. As the camp in 1939 was due about the middle of August, I selected two further weeks in September for my extra holiday. This was an unwise decision as events will show. As the date for camp approached, the T.A. unit to which we belonged asked for volunteers to proceed overnight as an advance party, by road, in lorries towing our guns behind. I discussed this with Jack and both being as green as grass; we broke the first rule in the soldier's code, Never Volunteer! We did!

With the B.E.F. to France

We climbed aboard an open lorry and took our seats on the floorboards behind the driver's cab. Our gun was fixed to the vehicle by an iron hook, at the rear. Together with a small similar convoy, the rest of the unit travelling in sensible comfort by train, we proceeded on our way to the camp at Beaulieu in the New Forest, near Southampton.

At first it seemed very adventurous, with the stars shining above in the dark blue sky of an August evening. Soon the slight drizzle which we had not foreseen developed and with no cover or protection of any kind, a long miserable night ensued. It began to turn cold – very cold – in the early hours of the morning as we drove through the countryside.

We were quite miserable and hungry by the time we arrived at a large field, covered with tents and a particularly large marquee, which did duty as a mass tent. We were allocated a tent and the two of us were given various equipment to store inside, so that there was just room for us to sleep. We were fortunate that our tent was situated on a slight rise on the ground, away from the main lines of tents.

Of that fortnight of camp, I remember the drills, lectures, fatigues, especially those spent in the mess tent, cleaning innumerable grease covered pans, being chivvied and chided for our poor efforts. We also marched along the beautiful country lanes that abound in the New Forest and I suppose that the first week of this very new experience passed reasonably well – until the rains came. The field became a quagmire. All the tents were flooded, except ours, where the water stopped just inside the entrance. Vehicles were bogged down in the thick gluey mud and had to be dug out, a most laborious task. Orders were given for us to evacuate this camp and we were all taken to a school at Farleigh, where the classroom floors provided dry accommodation and we had to accept the resulting disorganisation which endured until the end of the camp.

On my return home, I cannot say I was completely enamoured with my first experience of army life, but had the consolation of looking forward to the extra two weeks' holiday due to me in September. Unfortunately, the late unlamented Adolf Hitler, deemed otherwise, having invaded Poland, the war was about to commence.

My firm was packing up to leave Basinghall Street for Maidenhead where one of the partners was using his home as base for those older members of the small staff and it was considered would not be required for military service. I was busy helping with the preparation for departure, knowing full well that my dubious future was now in the precarious balance. The company informed me that, as a T.A. Member, I would obviously be called up and therefore stated that during my absence, my job would be left open for me and that my pay – less the 14 shillings per week the Army paid lowly gunners and private soldiers - would be sent to my mother. This pleased me tremendously, and I was extremely grateful for they kept this promise and more besides.

I received my blue call-up papers on 1st September 1939, shortly before war was officially declared and reported as ordered to Ennersdale Road. On arrival, I saw all our regiment thronging the parade ground on which we were set several tables containing piles of £1 notes. An officer at each table was in charge, and every lad proceeded when called, to approach the table, to receive £5 embodiment money, and to sign a form to indicate he was now a part of the regular British Army. On the tables were also piles of registered envelopes so that every person could, if he wished, send all or part of this vast sum to his dependants.

It was the most money I had ever seen, for £5 represented twelve hundred pennies, 240 to £1 and we could at that time purchase five cigarettes for two pence; or a better brand at three pence, 2 oz. bar of chocolate – two pence; pint of milk 1½ pence – pound of sugar 2 ¼ pence, or have a fairly good dinner in a cafe with sweet and cup of tea for one shilling – five pence. I immediately on receiving my £5 placed £1 in my pocket for emergencies and put £4 in a registered envelope, addressed to my mother.

After everyone had been paid and the registered letters had been despatched, the time was nearing 1.00pm and we were all informed that we would go home for lunch and return again at 2.30pm. I proceeded home, told my mother that the £4 would reach her soon in a registered envelope, had my lunch, said goodbye and returned to the depot.

Coaches had arrived on which all those not proceeding on vehicles with the guns and equipment were obliged to board, and off we set for Kempton Park Racecourse. We were only at Kempton Park for a month, but I remember it well. It had a railway platform inside the grounds, and we slept on the concrete floors of the various buildings, using the open perimeter as space for training purposes. I, as all the other lads, managed to get home one or two weekends, but most of our time was spent drilling and sundry chores called fatigues. I remember in particular the pay parade on Friday, where we would sit about the grassy ground, awaiting our names, always called alphabetically to ensure that if you were an 'S' like me and onwards, you would always be last to receive your pay. I had allotted my mother seven shillings a week from my pay, for if unfortunately, I did not survive, she would always receive that amount until the end of her days.

The old soldiers now joined us. These were men as opposed to our youthful selves. They had served in India for five or more years, had signed on the reserve, and were now duly obliged to repent for their sins. They were clad in ancient bedraggled uniforms for it was not until later; battle dress became a general issue. When I observed them, and knowing how strict the adjutant was on our morning parade, I expected to see the sparks fly. The adjutant, who also served in India, was quite sympathetic towards them and the obvious difficulties experienced by these old soldiers were never selected for onerous duties – but we were always chosen. I took a little time to learn. When a Sergeant enquired one day with a pleasant smile, if anyone could ride a bicycle, I of course leapt forward, to the amusement of comrades, and ended up cleaning the latrines.

Rumours were rife and colourful, besides being only a short war, for peace would ensure at any time, as it did all through the conflict, we the T.A. were the elite, and we would shortly be issued with tropical kit to proceed to our rightful station, Egypt. The regular army soldiers would return to take our place, do all the fighting required, and presumably join us behind the band in the parade of victory. This sounded extremely reasonable and re-assuring to me, especially as everyone except the old soldiers accepted this without question. I often think now, after the war, that there were professional rumour mongers paid to encourage the optimism that these sooth – Sayers pervaded.

We were all inoculated, the first indication that a move was imminent. Soon enough at the beginning of October, we were all ordered to prepare to leave in full marching order, carrying all equipment which one did, on one's back. We entrained at the railway station in Kempton Park en route for Southampton. On arrival at our destination, we were marched to the quayside where a troopship awaited. The army with extreme thoughtfulness, or perhaps it was some voluntary organisation, provided each man with an apple, pork pie (small) and a chocolate bar. We filed onto the troopship and tried to find space for ourselves upon deck, or below, for it was very crowded, with other regiments of the B.E.F.[1]

I was on deck and had been chosen by the usual army selection method to carry around my neck a heavy sling containing gun ammunition. Not being a muleteer, I was not keen on the additional harness.

We all settled down as best we could, scoffing our pork pie, etc, trying to peer through the darkness of the night, which had descended, but there was little to observe as blackout regulations were in force. After some hours, trying to settle and doze, although this was difficult as the night was cold, with a howling October gale, I spoke in a friendly way to the nearest individual. "Do you know the time?", "About 12.00pm." was the reply. "Oh good" I said hopefully, "I suppose we are nearly there".

[1] *British Expeditionary Force*

The figure grunted "You bloody fool, we're still in Southampton Harbour" he answered. Apparently, we were travelling to Cherbourg, which of course as everyone was aware, was not normally the route to Egypt.

Soon the engines sprang to life, and the ship cast off. We were on our way. We had not been going long when the old tub began to pitch and toss up and down in the heavy rough sea; it was no time at all before the lads were being sick, and not particularly caring upon whom. I managed to last out a little longer, but one pork pie finally got the better of me and I decided to go down below to use the toilets, to be sick. As I lurched to my feet, the ship seemed to climb up a tremendous wave, and then fall down on the other side. I was thrown across the ship hitting the rail, which knocked me flat. I tried to rise, noticing that the rail had a catch for opening, presumably to lower the gang planks if that ever again became likely to occur. I realised I was hampered by the belt of ammunition I was carrying, so promptly hurled this impediment as far as possible along the deck.

I staggered below to the toilets, which were well-lit. To my amazement the place was crowded with groaning, writhing, sea-sick bodies, some lying on top of the other. The stench of sickness was appalling, and I decided to meet my end upstairs on deck. It was a most awful experience, which seemed endless in our impotent misery, but at long blessed last, with the return of daylight we eventually sailed into Cherbourg.

We were all a sorry sight, dirty, and dishevelled, and I began to search for that wretched belt. I had no need to worry, for nobody in their right mind would have taken possession willingly of such an encumbrance. We disembarked under the curious eyes of the small contingent of French civilians and shore workers, who gazed askance at these representatives of the B.E.F. I began to feel a lot better now my feet were upon firm ground, and began taking an interest in all around.

Leading to Dunkirk and the beaches

From Cherbourg we proceeded as individual regiments to our rest camps. Ours consisted of old barn dwellings, where we slept on straw, using our blankets to cover us. It was sometime before everything was sorted out, and the Regiment put in full working order. After a few weeks consisting of innumerable drills, physical training, day manoeuvres and marches, it was decided that some men were superfluous to requirement, and I together with sundry personnel were sent down to Southern France, to a very pleasant place, named Pornichet. This I understood was not too far away from the Bay of Biscay and was a sandy cove, with cliffs not too high above the sea, with numerous pines and fir trees. There was a tented camp site where we were accommodated, eight men to one bell tent. I was fortunate that included in our tent were two elderly men, about 30 or more years of age, named Williams and Foster. Williams was an erudite schoolmaster, and Foster an educated scholar, who was always called the professor. They each wore spectacles, both portly gentlemen, Williams of medium height, Foster a little taller. They would have made excellent Pickwickians, had Dickens ever espied them, and in my opinion, were totally unsuitable for coping with the situation in which we were engaged. I liked them immensely and on asking them why they had volunteered for the war, they replied with enthusiasm that they only wanted to do their bit.

Each night by candlelight, Foster would read French newspapers to us, and Williams before retiring would solemnly kneel at the foot of his ground sheet and two blankets bed, clasp his hands together and pray. Foster would simply beam tolerantly at him and nobody in our tent would utter a word until he had finished. I admired Williams for his obvious sincerity, and the rest of the lads for their outward respect. On parade, each morning, they resembled Laurel and Hardy, dressed with their equipment, in various incorrect positions, covered sometimes with bits of straw, and cuts on their faces from shaving with very cold water.

I would sometimes of an evening in early November 1939 for the weather was still pleasantly mild, wander along the cliff road, with them, enjoying their intelligent conversation and often discussing the universe, our purpose upon Earth and other interesting topics.

Most of our time at Pornichet, was spent in marching, always marching; the usual camp fatigues, playing various games of football, and clambering over the rocky sandy shore. We were all classed as reserve material, and simply had to await our summons to re-join our units, if and when required. I remember vividly the accomplished bugler at that base, who played excellently every call throughout the day especially the Last Post in the evening. He excelled at Reveille, which was at an unearthly hour of 6.00 am but which we dare not ignore, and many choice epithets, were bestowed upon his rendition, also his forebears, etc.

The numerous rumour mongers were working hard, as usual and the most ominous one to assail our camp was the sinister information that we were all to be sent piecemeal to every Regiment of the B.E.F. except our own. This appeared to us to have an element of truth and would seem the natural organisation the army had from years of experience, perfected. Consequently, we waited anxiously each day for the dreaded news of our disposal.

Nearing Christmas, the call came for five lorry drivers to re-join our Regiment which was stationed in Northern France, at a place called Lomm, just inside the boundary of Lille. I had some learner driver experience on an army vehicle, which I had enjoyed, but never enough to be passed out as a competent driver. Nevertheless, on parade I immediately stepped forward as did four other hopefuls, and were accepted as fully trained drivers.

We departed the next day from Pornichet, armed with our rations, the ubiquitous tins of Bully Beef, with instructions to report to the Railway R.T.O for onward transmission to Lomm. We were all pleased to be going back to our old friends in the 91st Field Regiment and eagerly boarded a wooden seated, ancient carriage, drawn by an antiquated French Railway engine. Our progress was a series of starts and jolts, shunted from one place to another, and I am certain it took us three days to finally reach Lille. On arriving at Lomm we were assigned to the tasks for which we were needed. I was fortunately designated for H.Q. unit, and was informed together with another lad about my age, that we could choose between a motor-cycle despatch rider or a lorry.

I had no inclination or vaguest idea of how to handle an army motor-cycle, but my companion was falling over with excitement to have a go, on my declining. I was given a huge four or five-ton monster of a lorry, which I eyed with trepidation and ignorance. I should also mention that the weather in Northern France in December 1939 was bitterly

25

cold, with snow and ice. My co-driver was a regular experienced driver, who seeing my obvious reluctance to attempt to drive this mechanical contraption out of the Chateau, where it was now standing, through gates, only just wide enough to pass and onto the icy snow-covered road, which had tramlines along the middle, asked me, if I would like him to take it. I jumped at the offer, climbed into the spare seat, as my friend sat in the driver's seat and started up. We passed through the gates alright, and then started sliding slowly sideways across the road, towards the buildings on the opposite side. Despite my obvious alarm, my friend kept his head and we mounted the pavement and stopped without hitting anything. He looked at me cheerfully, "Ah, we need skid chains," he said thoughtfully. He jumped down, so did I and removed loads of steel chains from the back of the lorry. He fixed these chains, which I had never heard of, or ever seen in my life to each huge wheel, securing them over the tyres. We again set off slowly and proceeded to our destination where we had to collect some provisions.

We drove off the main road into a small road leading to a wide yard. The driver stopped the vehicle, looked at me, and cheerily enquired. "Would you like to have a go?"
I explained my inexperience and also nervousness to him but he said to try. So, I did. I started up correctly. I even engaged the gears and moved off up the road not too fast, into the yard. The only slight obstacle I had not imagined would exist in this snow-covered yard, were the two large iron bins, one of which I hit with the offside mudguard, which crumpled like brown paper. I stopped. I had to. Wringing my hands in horror, I alighted together with my co-driver, and surveyed the damage. My friend told me not to worry, and calmly

proceeded to kick the wing back into shape with his sturdy army boot. This not quite having the desired effect, he next seized a very heavy spanner from the vehicle tool box, and belted the wing into a vague shape. "There" he panted happily. "No one will notice it".

I was intensely relieved, and thanked him profusely. I also implored him to take the vehicle over himself, and accept me as his willing co-driver. To myself I decided at all costs to rid myself of this particular occupation.

I dropped gentle hints that although I was quite happy with a lorry, I was really more enthusiastic about orderly room, office work, typing etc, which really, I was not.

Strangely I am glad to say I was taken on as an orderly and given certain important duties. One was to remove all the wastepaper either in receptacles or on the floor, place this rubbish in a sack and then cart it across the road to an adjacent field, tip it out and burn it. Another task was to keep the boiler in the basement of the house where the H.Q. was located, constantly stocked up with fuel to ensure the radiators were sufficiently hot in the severe weather conditions. I had not been performing these tasks very long, when one day, an irate officer shouted down the stairs from his office on the first floor. "Orderly, why are these bloody radiators only warm?"

This remark was obviously addressed to me, and I heard it, in fact I did not consider it was cold, indeed I was sitting comfortably in front of the furnace, reading an excellent book and drinking a nice cup of tea. I hurried upstairs and felt the radiator, it seemed quite warm to me. I returned to the basement, grimly removing my battle-dress tunic, seized a shovel, opened the furnace door, and proceeded to shovel fuel into the roaring flames as fast as I could.

On top of the radiator was a dial with a red arrow, which I understood indicated danger if it swung over to the right. I hurled in the fuel, the needle swung over, the furnace boiler seemed to be rocking slightly, I decided it might be prudent to go upstairs and attend to other small duties. Sometime later, I had to go upstairs to the room where the officer had complained. He grunted as I crept in and placed some forms on his table. He was very red-faced, his tunic was undone at the top, and I saw perspiration on his forehead. He certainly seemed uncomfortable but merely glared at me, so I meekly withdrew.

When work had finished for the day, most of the lads would spend their evenings in Estaminets,[1] where drinks could be obtained; others would visit the houses of ill-repute and take their pleasures. They tried to persuade me to join them, but I would have none of that, not only did I eschew alcohol, but I was also fearful of being personally contaminated, and reluctant to confess I had no sexual knowledge of the female form; due to the segregated lives, we young men lived in peace-time. I was content to write letters home, read books, listen to the popular songs played over our little radio, which was a prized possession.

Leave to the U.K. had been underway for some time, and I impatiently awaited my turn which arrived in early March. I, together with a few other lads were given a good send off, on our way to Boulogne, where the leave boat sailed from.

[1] *A small café selling alcoholic drinks*

I remember Boulogne, a hill of cobbled stones leading down to the quayside, where the ship was decorated with little flags. Before boarding I had spent my remaining few Francs on cigarettes, which I had purchased from the N.A.F.F.I. I had some to give my brother, but most of my pay was spent on food, for I always seemed to be hungry. I had purchased a good old-fashioned breakfast from the N.A.F.F.I. of bacon, eggs and tomato's which should see me through the short see crossing Boulogne – Dover. I boarded the ship and found a place to sit on the deck. Everyone was happy and delighted to be going on leave. We waited and waited. After a very long time, it was announced that owing to fog in the Channel, the leave boat was unable to sail, would we return to our leave camp and try again tomorrow. The disappointment was intense, and out happy spirits disappeared as we marched back up the hill to the camp.

I suddenly realised I was broke, and had no money to buy food from the N.A.F.F.I, as none was otherwise provided. I also solved the problem of persuading the N.A.F.F.I. to accept my tins of cigarettes back in exchange for cash, and I was then able to obtain a meal that day, and breakfast the following morning. It did, but instead of 10 days leave I only received nine. Our crossing was uneventful, air cover was provided, by one aircraft, that was the only one I saw, and we reached Dover intact.

I thoroughly enjoyed my nine days leave with all my family, but too soon the day came for me to return, and my elder Brother, who was in a reserved occupation during the war, making airplanes, saw me off. It was the middle of March on my arrival back at Lomm, and a feeling of spring was in the air.

Parties of us were taken on a trip to Vimy Ridge, the scene of a tremendous battle in 1914-1918. Here I was visiting the place where young Thomas Dudley Ralph Shorrock had been killed in 1917. We were shown the opposing trenches which the French had made into a concrete memorial, and I understood there was miles of underground tunnels that had been constructed. At one point the trenches, German and British, were only a few yards apart. Our quartermaster took us on a tour of the tunnels and he himself had been at Vimy Ridge in 1914-1918. He showed us the exact spot where he slept during his time there, and I found it quite extraordinary that on this hallowed ground as he stood there, what memories he must have experienced. There was a large white memorial to the Canadians and British who had died at Vimy, and it was a very sad day for all of us to visit the ground where our Fathers had endured that terrible war.

The time began to fly by, through April to May, and then the Germans attacked through the Ardennes. The phoney war was over. We moved from Lomm up to the Belgian frontier, and from then on, all I can recall of that very short period, is constant moving, apparently, although I was unaware, rearwards. I remember the constant harassment, the seeming monopoly of German aircraft, Stukas, Dornier's. The need to scramble into trenches, the noise and confusion, never seeming to remain in one place for more than a few hours, even less. I had no idea what was happening, I remember the roads crowded with refugees, carrying or pushing in wheeled contraptions their pitiful possessions. In the book "The Week France Fell" there is a photograph of me sitting by the roadside on a grassy bank, with two civilians sheltering behind a tree. I remember that photograph being taken, whether by French or British Photographers, I do not know. I only know I pretended a nonchalance for their benefit, I certainly did not feel. I was amazed to discover that photograph a few years ago having obtained the book, quite by chance from my local library.[2]

We eventually came to a halt at a farmhouse which had a nearby duck pond. There were two or three of our vehicles parked near the pond, and we rest awaiting orders. When they were given, we could hardly believe our ears. The instructions were to render the vehicles unserviceable and retreat on foot to the coast about seven or eight miles away, carrying as little as possible. We complied with this command; our lorry driver put a pick through his radiator, and committed other damage to the engine. I threw my pack with all my spare clothes into the pond, as did the others. We were leaving nothing of any use to the enemy. Before we left I was given a broken attaché case full of military papers to take with me. The top of the case had come away completely and I was encumbered with the wretched case, which proved a thorough nuisance.

In my party, there were about ten men led by a Sgt Major, it was on the morning of 29th May 1940. We plodded grimly on over unploughed fields, crossing canals on wooden rickety, plank, makeshift bridges, stumbling in ditches, through hedgerows, on and on, saying very little to each other, every man overwhelmed by the seriousness of our situation. We finally came to a rough road lined with broken and burning army vehicles, left in a ruinous condition by the men who had gone before.

[2] A few years ago whilst watching a tv programme about WWII, I noticed that the photo was taken from film footage where my Grandfather was taking cover with fleeing refugees, from Stuka dive bombers.

Passing these until the end of the derelict line, we came to a rise in the ground, over some hillock, and reached the sea.

I did not know then where we were, but I soon discovered it was Bray Dunes, a vast sandy shore, stretching on my left for several miles to Dunkirk and again in an endless stretch to my right. I first saw the twin columns of smoke rising tremendously high into the sky, from the burning oil storage tanks at Dunkirk. To the left and right over the vast expanse of slightly sloping beaches, down to the sea, were thousands of English, French and possibly Belgian soldiers. A vast queue of men, three or four abreast, stretched from the top of the beach down to the sea, a distance of hundreds of yards. It was a very warm sunny day, with a clear blue sky, the sea appeared very calm, and immediately in front of my view, approximately ¼ mile from the beach, a large ship was slowly sinking bow first, with a third of the ship, the stern and propellers sticking out of the water. As I stepped onto the beach at the top, I saw immediately in front of me, lying on his back on the sand a dead British soldier, partly covered with a gas cape, and on top of his chest his army pay book, with his name written thus; Dvr Barraud R.A.S.C.

All this had only taken a few seconds to observe, when suddenly out of the blue sky came German Stuka dive bombers, hurtling down upon other ships who were busily loading troops from rowing boats, plying from the beaches. The scream of the sirens, which we know now were attached to these deadly aircraft, was awe inspiring, and although many brave lads stood their ground, on the beaches and fired their rifles at them, many of us, certainly myself threw ourselves desperately on the ground, endeavouring to appear as small as possible. I was amazed to see that only rowing boats manned by British sailors came into shore, from the transport, each boat holding a dozen men or more, if possible, then began the laborious task of rowing back to the ships, clambering up the sides, onto the deck, as the boats again returned.

I can only speak the truth as I witnessed these events, and as I joined the endless queue, with all men involved, there were constant dive-bomb attacks, with silver incendiary bombs falling all around the transports, many near misses but I am afraid many hits. I personally did not see any British aircraft over that part of the beach, in the two days I was there. I now know of the incredible bravery of the R.A.F, and throughout the war, but at that moment they were unfortunately, no doubt due to impossible demands upon them elsewhere, were as the saying goes, R.A.F. –Rare as Fairies. Neither did I see from that part of the beach any small motor launches or the little boats, that were widely used at Dunkirk, possibly this was due to the shallow water at the beach shore. It seemed all the evacuation was being carried out by a few, very few, not more than three or four long rowing boats.

We queued all that day in the heat, sheltering and reforming after every air attack. Far out to sea were flashes and the boom of gunfire from presumably capital ships supporting the attempts of the British valiant rear-guard holding the perimeter around Dunkirk, and adjacent beaches, in order to allow the evacuation to proceed. Over to my right were sand hills at the rear of the beach, and upon the highest was a French A.A. position, consisting of a light machine gun, manned by a couple of French sailors. They fired their gun continuously with apparently no shortage of ammunition at every air raid by the German planes. Despite these sterling efforts, I did not observe any aircraft shot down, although their effort must have been a morale booster in some respects. I, probably like many others, had nothing to eat or drink, nor could I remember the last time I had, with all the confusion and struggle to get so far. The rumours were around that we were going aboard these ships, to be landed somewhere in Southern France, at no time was I aware that these ships were heading for England.

That afternoon we gradually drew nearer to the water's edge. I was still clutching my precious case of papers, with which I had been saddled. During the late afternoon, the old paddle steamer, "Crested Eagle" appeared heading for the beaches about a mile over to my right. She stopped and lowered boats to ply to the shore to take on all the men she could carry. I had travelled on this ship many times from Greenwich Pier, down the Thames on trips to Southend, Margate and Clacton. She was one of a fleet of three steamers, the other being "Golden Eagle" and "Laguna Belle".

My father was friendly with the Captain of the "Golden Eagle" for it was on this ship that he travelled to France in the 1914-1918 war, and he pointed out to me the brass plate fitted to her deck, inscribed with the total of the many thousands of troops she carried to France without the loss of any men. The Captain of the "Golden Eagle" allowed my Father to visit him on the Bridge during the four-hour voyages. I spoke to a lad next to me, pointing out the "Crested Eagle" which was filling up with men, many having swum out to her, as with her low draught, she could get in fairly close. Suddenly the sound of planes again, and out of the sky, screaming vengefully down on the poor "Crested Eagle" came the dive bombers. I saw their silver incendiary bombs hit her, and she started to burn fiercely.

The lads on board were jumping over the side, in their efforts to escape the doomed vessel. We groaned for their awful plight, as the ship turned and ran aground on the shore in an effort, a most gallant attempt to save lives. Many chaps did survive, one of whom I met later in Stalag VIIIB, prison camp. He had the scars on his face, from the burns received before he managed to escape the flames. I should of course mention that the ship was too far away from us when she arrived at the beach, and there were also thousands of troops close by her, eagerly seeking to embark. The grounded, burning vessel lay on the strand with flames leaping from her, and she burnt on well into the darkness of that night, but did not attract any bombers, as possibly anyway she was a write-off or navigation at night in 1940 was not often attempted.

We at last reached the water, and stood behind our fellows in front, the water up to our knees would obviously go higher as the rowing boats came in. I regret to state that I saw one boat rushed, and the lads in it in grave danger of being precipitated into the sea. In the awful prevailing conditions of every man for himself, it was not unnatural that such an incident should occur. Whether this event triggered off the next incident, I do not know but suddenly just as it would have been our rightful turn to board the next returning rowing boat, an officer, with drawn revolver, leapt into the water, and ordered our party to the back of the queue, stating we had jumped the queue. This was incorrect, and quite understandably my party began to argue vigorously against this injustice. The officer threatened to shoot us. I think he meant it, so did the others. In despair, we left the water and tramped wearily up the crowded beach. It was at this point that I began to see little future in this operation. I hope I will be forgiven in view of the 300,000 men in total who were taken off the various beaches of evacuation.

I was tired, hungry, thirsty and decided to rest on the beach, as did the others. With the blessed relief of darkness, this would have been the best time to have left the beaches, for the cover of darkness gave us a welcome respite from the dive bombers. I fell asleep, and as it was a warm night I slept until the first glimmering of daylight. Then I discovered I was alone. The remaining lads I was with had disappeared - they had got off the beach. They made it back, how I do not know, possibly by raft or maybe in the darkness they managed to get on a boat of some kind. They thoroughly deserved their good fortune by their persistence. I was now alone, surrounded by thousands of troops whom I did not know.

As I again joined the queue, and of course fellows were coming onto the beach from other regiments all the time, increasing the already crowded shore. I saw a friendly face, at least I recognized one man, named King, belonging to our regiment. He had just arrived on the beach, and was probably one of the rearguards. I called him and he came over to me.

"What are you doing here, you should have gone by now". he told me.

I explained the situation to him, also the fact that I could only swim a few strokes, and the transports were further out, deceptive to the eye.

"I am going to swim out" he said grimly.

He removed his uniform and boots, leaving them in a pile on the sand and with quick purposeful strides reached the sea, plunged in and swam away. I watched him wistfully, admiring his resolution and courage, yet reluctant to say goodbye to a friendly person.

If a transport was lucky enough to get as many men aboard her as possible and if the Luftwaffe gave them only near misses, they set sail as fast as possible. That meant there were periods when our section of beach seemed to be devoid of ships. We of course were only a portion of the thousands seeking rescue. I glanced over to my right again at the smoking burnt-out hulk of the poor old "Crested Eagle" and patiently waited and waited to get to the water again. It was a long, long time since King had departed and then I suddenly saw him staggering along the beach, and leaving the queue, as no ships were in sight, I rushed over to him. He was completely exhausted. When he had sufficiently recovered, he muttered to me.

"It's a bloody long way out there, further than you think". After he had rested for a while, he went off to look for his clothes.

It was now the early afternoon of the second day which I hope was 30th May, but owing to the nightmare that had been taking place I cannot guarantee the accuracy of the exact day. I know it was very hot and I was beginning to feel a foreboding of ultimate disaster. Over to my left was a Major sitting on the sand surrounded, I correctly assumed, by men of his Regiment. I approached him, explaining myself, and showing him my case of military papers. I broached the possibility of perhaps being captured by the Germans if the beaches were overrun, and sought his advice. He perused the papers, sorting them into two piles, one of which he told me to burn, which I did then and there. The other pile he replaced in the battered case, and told me to bury it in the sand, which I did by scooping a fair-sized hole from the soft sand. I felt a lot better having rid myself of my unwanted burden, and also the vague fear that if I had been captured with these even innocuous documents, what would be the reaction of my captors.

All this time the usual mayhem continued unabated, the Navy firing out from the sea, the bombers seeming to own the skies, plenty of noise. I sat down on the sand not far from the Major and his group for a little while, when from that section a L/C Taplin approached me He was a pleasant young man, a little older than myself, very smart considering the conditions we were experiencing. I also noticed he had a small moustache. He spoke to me.

"I see you are on your own. The major had suggested we try and form ourselves into little groups of 50 men or so, spread out, and suggests we try to burrow as best we can, a hole each for ourselves - he paused. The major is trying to organize most of the chaps in this way."

I readily agreed, I was only too happy to be part of a community of any sort.

"By the way" said L/C Taplin, "Have you had anything to drink, sorry we have no food, but we have just managed to brew some tea, without sugar or milk".

I thanked him fervently for this was a splendid piece of luck for me. I busily scooped out a small hole, which I am afraid my 6'2" did not fit into at all.

He returned with a white enamel mug half full of delicious tea. I took it gratefully as he returned to his place. I put the cup to my lips, it was hot, it was marvelous, when suddenly without any warning, a shell landed right into the group in front of me.

Wounded, in hospital

There were screams from the wounded, as more shells arrived on the groups of men. The Germans were in artillery range behind us which was an ominous sign. Men began to run for the shelter of the sand hills to my right just below the French Light A.A. machine gun post. The Major leapt to his feet and shouted. "Don't run, stay where you are. Don't panic, stay down". I had to make a decision. I was inexperienced just 20 years of age on 15.5.1940. I decided to take my chance and run for the sand hills. I got to my feet and clearly recall running, falling flat as the shells whined over. I did this three or four times, drawing nearer almost to the small hills, suddenly the next shell which I heard, and instantly got down, seemed to burst above me and I felt stunned. I tried to get on my feet, which I did, knowing there was something terribly wrong.

I looked down at my battle dress tunic which was turning red with blood. I knew I had been hit, and realized it was in the back. As I staggered forward, two soldiers rushed at me getting me to the cover of the small sand hills. They took off my tunic, and as they did so I pulled out of my trouser pocket the emergency field dressing bandage, which was always impressed upon us to retain for our use. These gallant lads quickly bandaged my wound, but one of them tore his own field dressing from his pocket to add to mine. I must have been still dazed for I said to him.

"You are not supposed to use your dressing on my wound".

He merely ignored my words and continued to bandage me. A Frenchman rushed down from the A.A. position, he was wearing the white and blue striped, light jersey of the French Navy, and wore a blue beret on his head. He helped me along with my other two friends towards a large French Sanatorium which was so close to the beach that the iron railings set in cement were actually at the beginning of the beach.

The hospital was built of red brick and had wards built in a semi-circular fashion on ground floor level. As we approached many of the lads were lying along the concrete base below the railings with their rifles at the ready, and I thought it was a magnificent sight, that only the British could possess this stolid defiance in the face of appalling adversity. They glanced up at me sympathetically as I was helped along, and something about their expressions caused me to shout. "Good luck, lads". They replied with curses on the Fuhrer, the Germans and their ancestors. I felt a terrific pride in my comrades and their solid determination and courage.

I entered the hospital and went into a large room that had no windows. It was lit by a single light swinging from the ceiling, the bulb covered by a green shade. The whole floor was covered with hardly any available space by wounded men on stretchers. With their groans of pain, the building was vibrating to the thud of gunfire, screaming aircraft, and the British Naval Guns far out at sea hurling their projectiles over towards the enemy. I was placed face down on a stretcher to await my turn to be taken into the operating room, which I felt was a makeshift one, as the entrance was opposite me and men were being carried in at intervals. I thought to myself that if ever there was a hell upon Earth that I had probably found it. My friends had of course returned to the beach outside and I saw two elderly Sisters of Mercy hurrying about the room comforting the wounded. One of these Sisters had tears streaming down her face and I felt so sorry for her that she should have to endure this horror also.

As I tried to swivel my head round to see the whole of this room, or as much as possible, I saw a French Priest dressed in full religious clothes with a purple sash around his neck, and a crucifix suspended also. He was, I thought a Roman Catholic Father. I am of course C of E. He was very calm and human. He approached many stretchers and made the sign of the cross over those lying on them. I became apprehensive as he worked his way towards me. Straining my neck until it ached, I knew he was behind me and I saw the slow deliberate sign of the cross placed over me, from the shadow afforded by the light. I called out, "no, no, not me, not me." The Priest moved to the front of my stretcher smiled not understanding my outburst and he patted my head gently and moved on. I groaned inwardly. He must know, I thought, he can see perhaps the state of my wound, even with bandages roughly applied. So, this was it, after all this. I must have been exhausted for I went out like a light.

Sometime later I came to, just as I was being lifted on to the operating table. In those few seconds of time I saw two French surgeons with rubber aprons which were covered with blood. I saw two large Oxygen bottles, from which a rubber tube fixed to one of them was joined by a large black bladder, going in and out, and the rubber tube coming from the other side of the bladder to join a thick rubber black mask. I had seen a similar contraption when as a young boy, I had two teeth removed by gas. I did not like that experience at all and resolved never to undergo that sensation again.

One of the French doctors said in English, quite plainly, he was the one holding the mask close to my face.

"You will sleep".

I replied instantly.

"Not likely". I started to try to get off the table, but the French doctor had no time or inclination to soothe panic stricken victims. I do not know what force they used - only - that the mask smacked into my face, that I was almost breathless and struggled to breathe, inhaling the gas. I remember the buzzing, the noise, it was the most horrible nightmare I had ever known. It must have been the evening when I regained consciousness and found myself in a large long ward, with every bed occupied by wounded men. I could not focus at first and must have been delirious for a time, for faces of people who looked at me seemed to grow larger and smaller. Finally, the scene cleared then I found to my surprise and anguish I was lying on my back enduring such pain. I had to get onto my side to alleviate this and a French lady nurse who was trying to understand my babbling did not comprehend that I needed to turn over in bed. Somehow, I managed, at last after some effort, to achieve this then as I lay thankfully on my left side, I gazed at the occupant of the next bed. It was L/C Taplin. He gave me a friendly smile, asking me how I was. I told him and enquired where he was wounded.

He took his good arm from under the sheet and I saw with sadness and horror that he had lost his other arm completely right to the shoulder. I was stunned. The chap who had befriended me, pouring me that wonderful mug of tea that I never managed to finish.

I now urgently required the toilet which was situated at the end of the ward. I found it quite impossible to use the bottle provided for this purpose and knew somehow, I had to make the attempt to reach the toilet. With great difficulty and pain, I managed to climb out of bed and slowly hobble, almost crawl to reach my goal. Having once completed the task I decided to do that every time. My wound was dressed each day by the doctor and nurse, as I lay on my stomach gritting my teeth, for the pain was intense.

It was now either the 1st or 2nd June 1940, and the noise outside was still shaking the many glass windows of our ward, which I expected to shatter at any moment. We could see through our window, the next long semi-circular ward full of patients. Whether it was on this day or 3rd June, I am not sure, but I was lying in my bed chatting to L/C Taplin, when a shell landed slap in the middle of the next ward, followed by another. It was horrible, the glass in our ward shattered, and the resultant pandemonium from the helpless wounded was unbearable. There was smoke, debris and screams coming from the ward that was hit and we had no way of knowing if further German shells would next land in our ward. L/C Taplin looked at me and said "I'm afraid this is it he grabbed my hand with his good one and went on. "I'm putting my head under the pillow, Goodbye".

I wished him a fervent goodbye and did the same. We remained like that for a very long time, then each of us cautiously withdrew our heads breathlessly awaiting events.

Our French doctor and nurse had rushed over to the damaged ward, which must have been a terrible sight for when the next time I saw them, it was plain to see from their faces what they had experienced. Things began to quieten down, the noise was gradually abating, soon to be replaced by an ominous silence. I had previously, before the shelling of the next ward, asked the French doctor who spoke very little English, if there was any way I could get back on to the beaches, knowing really in my heart, in the condition I was, that it must have seemed a ridiculous suggestion. The doctor however made enquiries for me, to return later and say that it was terrible on the beach and out of the question for me to attempt to rejoin those gallant lads.

Captured, journey to Germany

It was I think about the 6th June and the quietness, with no sound of diving aircraft, could mean only one thing - that it was all over. I prepared to make one of my trips up the ward, also to see another English lad who had a serious leg wound and had lost part of the other leg. Incidentally, there were only the three of us in that ward. I looked out of the window on to the small pathway between the wards and saw, with very mixed feelings, a middle-aged German soldier slowly riding along on a bicycle. I knew what that meant so very quickly pointed this out to L/C Taplin. We knew that it was over, that we were now Prisoners of War.

Later on, that day about mid-morning there entered, into our ward at the far end, plain to every person who was able to see, two German officers, or perhaps one and a Feldwebel (Sergeant). We did not know their ranks at that time of course. They proceeded down the ward accompanied by the French doctor, to whom they were addressing questions. They stopped at the first English boy with the wounded legs, for a brief moment, again at L/C Taplin's bed and then they came face to face with me. As I gazed at them with curiosity with I suppose an unfriendly look, the French doctor explained my condition. The German officer bellowed out the first, but certainly not the last Teutonic word I ever heard. Raus! Raus! Raus! Out! Out! Out!

In a very short time clothes were brought to me for I had no possessions, no underclothes, only the hospital shirt or shift I was wearing. My meagre belongings had disappeared on entering the hospital. I examined my new uniform with reluctance. They consisted of a reasonable pair of French army boots, which fitted me, a pair of khaki trousers, which reached some distance above my ankles and from whose army or period I could not imagine. A pair of blue and white striped socks, a presumably Belgian or French tunic, vintage 1914-1918, a similar forage cap, with a red tassel. The last item was the blue and white striped light French jersey, traditionally worn by French sailors. I had no underclothes and no option but to put on this music hall outfit.

When I was dressed I looked at L/C Taplin. Despite the gravity of the situation, he could not disguise his laughter at the sight. I had to join in, knowing that I was leaving him and would probably never again see him. There was little time for farewells as the impatient Germans came and shepherded me out of the ward. I never saw or heard of L/C Taplin again, but if he ever reads these lines I know he will remember.

Outside the hospital were ambulances to take all selected personnel away. In the ambulance, I was allocated, all sitting down persons, everyone was French and I looked like a Frenchman, or at least like one who had been shipwrecked on a remote island for some time. I tried to make them understand I was English, but they advised me in sign language to keep quiet so I did. We drove off, and some miles later we ended up at a French hotel, at Hesdin.

It was now being used to accommodate POW mainly in fact all French officers and other ranks. It was only a hotel in outward respects, inwardly it was just a place taken over for sleeping as many soldiers as possible. It was quite good compared to anything I was later to experience. I was placed in a room which contained five camp beds, four Frenchmen and myself.

The food was not bad at all compared with later places, it consisted of two meals a day. Black coffee; sugar and milk less in the morning, at mid-day we lined up in the kitchens to receive a plate containing a ladle of mashed potatoes, some slices of meat or sausage, possibly there were carrots or some other vegetable. We were also given a chunk of French bread and we had wine or water which of course I chose to drink. This same meal was again served at about 5.00 pm I was always hungry for I could not seem to make up for the lack of food over the previous weeks.

We had nothing to do but mingle in the hotel grounds in the beautiful summer weather in June. The place was very crowded, but I saw sitting on the grass three English lads, one was a fair-haired lad from an anti-tank regiment and had been wounded in the foot. His companions were from his regiment and I listened as I approached them eager to join them. The fair-haired boy had an educated accent and was talking to his friends as I gazed at them. They stopped speaking looking at me, then one lad turned to the other and clearly said.

"What's that bloody peculiar froggy staring at us for".

I immediately told them I was English and they laughed at my get-up. They all had their own British battledress uniforms, this is something I would have to endure.

The days passed slowly and we were all anxious for news, for we knew now although the French were still fighting, and our B.E.F. was evacuated to England, the French could not survive much longer. One day I was walking slowly downstairs to go out to the grounds, which of course were surrounded by improvised barbed wire and patrolled by many German sentries, when I saw a French officer with tears streaming down

48

his face, jabbering away to everyone he saw. Instinctively I knew France had fallen.

This was later confirmed so now we were alone isolated. I had received no news from home since a birthday card from my family, which I received about 20th of May. I worried about them and what was happening at home, realising too that they could not know of my misfortune. The other three English lads had been trying to persuade the Germans to send us all to an English hospital which was located at Camiers. I was as enthusiastic as they to go imagining that it would be a haven with better food and conditions.

How wrong we were, for the Germans did move us to Camiers, possibly because it was further inland away from the sea. Camiers proved to be a very big disappointment. Not only was the food very sparse far little than we had been receiving but there was a complete absence of cigarettes which affected nearly everyone.

There were many British soldiers at Camiers recovering from their wounds, so we had at least the consolation of discussing all the events with one another. I was also able once again to obtain regular dressings each day to my back, which was very sore and tender and I still retain the large scar to this day.

I considered the treatment at Camiers harsh. The medical Sgt. in charge of our ward constantly harried us and one day ordered three of us to scrub the long corridor outside. In spite of my weakness and the pain in my back, he bullied us into trying to perform this onerous task. I made a mental resolve to bring this matter to the attention of the Army Authorities on my return home. I never knew that the subsequent events and years would drive this intention from my mind, but I certainly recall it now. I had been at Camiers some ten days or a fortnight, and was told I had some longer period of convalescence due, before I would be considered fit.

The Germans ordered all of those who could walk, out of the hospital for the march to Germany and captivity. I had to go but managed to get hold of a light blanket, which I secured to my body with a piece of string. This was a most sensible thing to do as events would show. I only wish I had my water-bottle, and the opportunity to fill it, and to try to keep it filled. Those lads who did this were indeed fortunate and sensible. We paraded outside the hospital in a long column of three ranks. With numerous guards either side of our column we set out on the infamous march to Germany that most members of the captured B.E.F. had to endure.

This march, which would take us over a fortnight through France, and Belgium to Holland in the desperate heat of that very hot summer of 1940, is engraved on the memories of those who took part. We used to commence marching very early in the morning as soon as daylight, 4 or 5 o'clock. We had to march until 3 or 4 pm in the afternoon. Feeding arrangements were virtually remote and negligible. As we proceeded over the hot dusty roads thousands of Frenchmen were far in front of the English troops and consequently fared much better in obtaining food and drink from their fellow countrymen en route. Nevertheless, the French civilians were very good to us also and in every village or hamlet we passed, they were waiting, women in particular, to provide pails of water by the roadside, and to push or throw bread, or whatever they could spare into the hungry columns of men.

The German guards who accompanied our column were vicious and nasty. I do not think they were the front-line troops but older men possibly of 1914-18 war service. They would hit, kick and punch anyone who broke ranks, as many did to snatch the food.

They would kick over the pails of water so that we were unable to obtain a drink. They would use their rifle butts at every opportunity, but were experts at using their feet as well. I had to be extremely careful for if I tried to break ranks to obtain food, many others did also. I often got a shove in the back in the ensuing melee, which caused me great pain. I also had to ensure that no guard hit my back with his rifle so I was constantly on the alert. Consequently, the opportunities for me to obtain food were few and far between and although the lads would share with you occasionally, they were in the business of survival themselves, and could not afford to be over generous.

Every afternoon we would halt at barns or other accommodation the Germans could find. If not, we had to spend the night in the open and my blanket became very useful to have. After each day's march, I had to find someone to dress my back. There were medical orderlies who had been captured who provided this service if they had any medical supplies left. One time I was actually treated by a correct German medical officer who spoke not a word to me in the process. Getting my wound attended was a constant problem, which was to plague me for some weeks to come.

After a few days on the march I suffered weakness which I am sure was caused by lack of food. This resulted in a pain in either groin, which caused me great difficulty in marching, compelling me to fall out to rest often along the roadside. Hundreds of men did this for various reasons if not sheer tiredness. The French were notorious and dropped out at every opportunity. In the ranks of the French were very many squads of Black Senegalese or Zouave, troops, who would sit at the roadside with their heads in their hands in an attitude of deep despair. The ruthless German guards had a remedy for this situation, and would start swinging their rifles at the beginning of the line of seated soldiers, who endeavored to rejoin the march, if quick enough to dodge the blows. Some were able, but I saw many clubbed in this fashion.

I used to warily eye the advancing rifle swinging maniacs until I judged it time to get up. I then plodded wearily after the main column now receding in the distance. We did not realize then that the Germans employed an old trick of sending a couple of motorcycle combinations up and down the road, with the well-armed sub-machine gun occupant of the side-car ever vigilant. They would often pass us coming and going giving the impression that the marching route was well patrolled by troops. It was intended to discourage any escapers by this method. There was of course German military traffic using the roads from time to time which all helped to promote this illusion.

On a hot sunny afternoon, late in June 1940, I staggered along the road seeming to be almost alone. I was merely putting one foot after the other. The tree lined road vanished ahead in the distance. I could see no column of troops or a guard in sight.

I stopped to rest and at that moment from behind me riding at a slow place, was an elderly German soldier on a bicycle. He pulled up in front of me, making signs as though to enquire

52

why I was all alone on the road. He looked quite a human sort of person not like the other guards marching with the column. I rightly suspected his job was to round up the genuine stragglers. In the few French words I knew, I tried to explain that I was wounded in the back and showed him my dressing. I also pointed to my thighs, trying to explain my walking problem. Whether he thought I had been wounded in several places I do not know, but he bade me to sit down and rest.

We remained there for a while and then I heard the approach of a German lorry. The guard stood in the roadway and raised his hand. The vehicle ground to a halt. The guard motioned me to get up and accompany him to the rear of the lorry which was covered in. He then let down the tailboard, pulled aside the flaps, to reveal forms either side of the truck on which comfortably seated were about ten French soldiers, looking remarkably refreshed. The guard spoke to them in German and it was quite obvious to me, from the word "Komerad", that they should move up to afford me room to clamber in. The French merely muttered among themselves and did not budge an inch.

My kindly German guard changed in a flash. Screaming in German, he unslung his rifle, grabbed the barrel with both hands; brought it down with such force on the rear side form, that the occupants leapt up and ended in a heap behind the driver's cabin. There was now enough room for half a dozen men. The guard turned to me reverting immediately to his kindly manner and assisted me into the lorry. I was grateful. I thanked him, and off we went. The French ignored me, they were still getting over the shock. I was secretly quite pleased.

We travelled mile after mile in marvelous style arriving at the open field where we were to spend the night, with all the other exhausted marching prisoners. Now I had to forage for food, get my back dressed and get to sleep. I started to consider the circumstances of my lorry ride and came to the conclusion that the artful French were using this method to avoid marching. Well two can play at that game. The next day's march was easier now I knew what to do. After a mile or two let the column disappear, start to stagger along, which was more natural than assumed, await the sound of a German lorry, act in a bad way, raise the right hand hopefully and there I was. It works, but not every time, for the cunning Germans either did not send a follow-up lorry to collect the stragglers, or had given up the idea. Still I had enormous help for when I did ride I overtook the main column and arrived hours ahead. The bliss of that journey was a boost to my morale.

In this manner, we eventually reached the Dutch border and there we were placed in little goods wagons attached to an engine where we all stood and could see easily over the top. The little train pulled away chugging through fields, streets and countryside, until at last we arrived at a wide canal where numerous barges were waiting.

Each man was handed a large Dutch loaf as he walked up a small gangplank. The loaf was about a foot or 18" in diameter. All the loaves were stale and mildewed, with green patches in them, but it was a huge loaf, and I grabbed mine ravenously, and began wolfing the bread as did many other lads. We were all put down into the hold of the barge where it was dark and tremendously hot. We did not know that the loaf of bread was intended to last each man three days. When all the barges were full we moved off along the canal and of course there were demands from all the men in the hold to be allowed on deck to relieve themselves. The hatch above the hold was not shut, but a wooden ladder was used to enable us one at a time to go on deck for toilet, but more hopefully to get some fresh air. Arriving on deck I saw either side of the canal for miles was populated by relaxed, sun-tanned German troops, with music from gramophones playing, laughing, eating, enjoying themselves. We had to urinate straight over the side in full view of the Germans or girls. To do the other business a wooden cradle was suspended either side of the barge upon which one had to sit exposing one's bottom to all and sundry. These cradles could accommodate half-a dozen men at a time either side of the barge.

On the second day of our canal journey we reached a wider part of the canal, and halted. Chugging towards us I saw a motor launch containing German soldiers and a Dutch civilian doctor. The launch stopped beside the barge to allow the doctor to board.

The wounded were told to queue up for treatment, which I and several other chaps did. When I reached the doctor, he appeared to be a pleasant man about 40 years of age. I remember he was dressed in a brown coat, such as shop assistants wear. He smiled at me and carefully dressed my back. On completing his work, he looked around quickly to note where the guards were, before slipping into my pocket a wonderful gift, a small bar of chocolate. This little kindness heartened me considerably, demonstrating the regard for us by the Dutch people. At long last the wretched three-day journey came to a close. Leaving the barges, we were marched for quite some distance to a large field, containing several water-troughs.

Here for the first time we were able to clean ourselves, as best we could with cold water, but we were now in the grip of a savage tormentor, for we were all thoroughly lousy. Lice live and breed on the body, biting and drawing blood, invading every part especially those covered with hair. We constantly scratched and scratched, but these lice concealed themselves in seams of uniforms and the only way to destroy them was to light a candle if one was available, and go over the seams burning them out. This did not destroy the eggs which hatched out many more of these vile vermin. It would take almost a year to finally rid ourselves of these pests. After a night at this field, we marched off again in the morning, for we were now just inside the border of the fatherland, and ready to receive our first taste of German culture. As we approached a village, the inhabitants were all lined up ready to receive us, nearly all old men, young and old women and the detestable children. As we passed this happy crowd; they hissed, and spat upon us; tried to kick us, unrestrained in their affectionate welcome by the sadistic guards. I was very pleased I was again marching in my favourite position in the middle of the rank of three abreast, this I always adopted if possible thus having a lad on either side to offer some protection from a blow in the back.

We soon reached railway sidings, where a long goods train was awaiting to transport us. The French contingents had long ago left us and only the British were now at this spot. The guards herded us with kicks and blows into the goods wagon. 50 men were crowded in each of these cattle-trucks in intense heat, with no water or food for a five-day journey to Silesia, destination Lamsdorf, Stalag VIIIB, near the Polish border.

Arrival at Lamsdorf, Stalag VIII - First working party

The doors of our cattle-truck were shut and locked, the guards boarding a coach attached to the front of the train, or if a coach was not available, they had a cattle-truck to themselves, with the door always open, so they could watch for any escape attempts. The heat in my truck was unbearable for we were sitting close up, unable to stretch our legs except when standing. Many lads were unwell and had to urinate or most unfortunately empty their bowels for which no provision had been made. Consequently, a nauseating smell permeated the hot wagon so I consider this journey was the worst one we had to endure. The train was often shunted into sidings, or stopped for long periods, but we were only allowed out for a short time once a day. We were unable to obtain water except possibly once or twice in the five days. This was the most terrible hardship, which even those who had brought full water bottles into the wagon suffered from. I remember the awful thirst vividly for I remember one soldier who had a water bottle and would share with no one. I had nothing to drink, but he cracked first, moaning all the time for water, which was not to be had. At last this nightmare journey ended at the small station of Lamsdorf, and we thankfully detrained under the watchful eyes of our shouting, cursing, guards. We were lined up in threes and off we marched the few miles to reach our home base, for the next five years.

On our way to Stalag VIIIB, the road led through a pine tree wood bordering each side. On the left-hand side were clearly visible the crosses of the graves containing previous prisoners of war, that the Germans had held in 1914-18. This was a grim reminder of the uncertainty of our future and we all fell silent, as we marched past that gloomy place. As we reached the camp we saw it had been built on a wide flat area, surrounded by forests of pine trees. The first sight was of the high barbed wire perimeter fence round the huge square of the camp. We saw the four watch-towers, tall posts constructed to support a small shed on top of the four posts, with a wide opening all round the shed and the machine gun mounted to fire if required. Each box was built in the same way. As we approached the main gate manned by sentries it opened to reveal many compounds each containing several long barracks with white adobe walls.

We were all taken to a large dispersal area where tables had been placed at the end. Every man was searched thoroughly, queued up at the tables where fingerprints were taken, details written down, not only for German records, but in order to supply information to the Red Cross of name, Regiment, Number of captured POW. Our heads were shaved very close to the scalp probably serving various purposes, one that in the event of escape, we could be easily spotted among civilians, second to curb the lice, we all had. The final stage in this virtually all-day procedure was to place a board around each person's neck suspended by rope, bearing the camp number painted in white on the black background. We were then arranged with our boards in suitable groups, for our photograph to be taken. My number was Kriegsgefangener No. 17063. (POW No. 17063).

We were now officially registered as British POW's and as such under the Geneva Convention via the Swiss Red Cross entitled to that treatment according to the agreed Rules of Warfare, to which Germany had signed. In other words, if the Germans shot you for any reason or whim of their own, they ought to notify the Red Cross. After the completion of these formalities we were taken in groups to our various compounds. Before being assigned to our barracks we were addressed by a sun-tanned German called "South American Joe". He had apparently resided in South America, before returning to link his destiny with the Third Reich. He pointed out to us the trip wire which was set back a few feet from the barbed wire fence. Crossing that without the permission of the appropriate guard in the watch tower, would risk being shot. Besides the usual harangue, informing us to obey all their rules, this German ended his discourse with the famous words.

"You will now go into your barracks and receive a meal of potatoes, fish, soup, bread, butter and jam."

We the very hungry perked up at this news, until we heard the perambulating prisoners whisper to us as they passed, "Wait till you see it".

We entered our barrack which was a long low building, on one side by the windows with their wooden shutters were several tables and forms spaced along the concrete floor. On the other side in uniformity were three-tiered bunk beds, each bed comprising several slotted bed boards, which supported a straw palliasse. The tiers of beds backed onto one another and spaces between tiers were approximately a yard in width. Each half of the barracks contained when completely full about 150 men. In the middle section of the barrack there was a water trough with cold water taps only for ablutions. Passing through the washroom brought a prisoner into the second half of the barrack, containing a similar number of tiered beds.

The latrines in each compound of four barracks, were situated about 20-30 yards from the nearest barracks. They had entrances either end, were constructed of wood, beside the usual stand-up wall urinal, had another section with black continuous wooden box frame, with about 10 circular holes, and a similar arrangement opposite. These were earth closets and were emptied regularly by a man with a horse and cart, the cart consisting of an enormous wooden barrel, to which was attached a suction hose, and was hand-pump operated. The sewage was conveyed outside the camp, not very far from the outer wire, and pumped or emptied into a sewage farm. These latrines were covered over with a wooden roof and had wooden walls with windows. Each man on entering a barrack was given the minimum number of bed boards, an empty palliasse, which had to be filled by him with straw, at a place provided within the camp. In each barrack in the corridor space between the rows of wooden tables and tier-beds were two widely separated tiled heating stoves but very little heat was obtained due to the totally inadequate fuel supplied.

To return to the time we had entered the barrack, selected our beds on mutual agreement in most cases with our comrades, or by first come first served; fixed our bed boards, filled our palliasses; and were now to enjoy our first delicious meal.

This consisted of half a Dixie,[1] or most probably 1/2 of a Dixie of watery soup, which stank of putrid fish. Floating in this almost clear liquid were minute pinhead portions of white matter. We also received per man four or five small boiled potatoes with black rotten portions inside most of them. We were also provided with a square piece of German bread of about two slices, on top of which was placed either a ½ inch square of Ersatz (Substitute), Margarine or a teaspoon of Ersatz Jam, or a round piece of yellow stinking cheese about two inches in diameter.

A full day's ration would be, early morning, a mug full of black coffee made from acorns, without of course sugar and milk. This was served about 6.30-7.00 am. each morning. The soup was brought to every barrack about 11-12 noon with the potatoes and at 3.00-3.30 pm the bread ration was distributed. This in my opinion was barely enough to keep one alive and after the first few days of this diet, I soon realized something had to be done to augment this food supply. Our day began with early morning roll-call where we would go outside into the compound, every barrack complement parading in ranks of three.

There was always a welcome performance by the guards when counting the ranks of men, but finally the count was agreed, after a few minutes. Then we had the rest of the day to sit about and dream constantly of food and cigarettes, virtually unobtainable, except for the lucky few who had managed to keep supplies.

[1] *A metal tin and cooking pot with a folding handle*

Paper was extremely scarce and this caused great hardship when using the toilets, particularly as most of us had looseness caused by the coarse food, water supply, and other factors. There were a few prisoners who possessed paperback books and those who had bibles also. All these gradually were sacrificed in the last resort to the call of nature. One young lad I saw with a paperback book was reading avidly and I approached him to ask if I could borrow the book, when he had read it. He replied that he was sorry, but was compelled to dash for the toilet so frequently that it was a race against time to try and finish reading the book.

I would have to remain in my ridiculous uniform for a long time before sufficient supplies of clothing arrived through the Red Cross. In the meantime, my French boots were worn out, as were those boots of very many other prisoners. The Germans issued to the Sgt's. or Sgt. Majors of each barrack, foot rags, being a piece of grey linen about a foot square. These were used as a substitute for socks and were intended to protect our feet from the chafing of the clogs, with which every prisoner had been provided. Very many of these were the Dutch wooden clogs, but there were also many with a hard composite upper. These clogs were extremely uncomfortable in which to walk, work or to relax in. It was a common scene to observe men hobbling or shuffling along.

It was now August 1940. As I sat down outside the barrack on the ground with my back to the wall, to enjoy the benefit of the very hot sunshine and hopefully to attempt to mitigate the hunger pangs. I noticed that on standing up I would get a little giddy, not only from lack of food, but also due to weakness, for I was very thin. My back still required dressing, but now there were facilities in the camp, with our own captured British medical staff, who had very little medical supplies available.

Outside the main camp and a short walk through the woods, a hospital for the sick and those requiring surgical treatment was being organized for the more serious cases. This hospital was under the control of our own medical officers, monitored by the Germans, who naturally escorted every patient to and from the hospital.

Many more prisoners were coming in as they completed their journeys to Stalag VIIIB. A separate compound was used for the R.A.F. of whom at present the Germans had very few captives, mainly those who flew on the leaflet dropping raids in September / October 1939, and had been shot down. These were our long serving POW's with almost a year to their credit, and were the envy of no one.

Every prisoner was discussing the chances of going to work to obtain extra food and in order to escape the grim living conditions of the camp. They all wanted to work on farms where they imagined food would be more plentiful. The Germans used this to their advantage in taking would be farmers instead to the coal mines. Although the coal mines were not as dangerous to work in as the British mines, I had no intention of ending up down one, for although the rations were far better than anywhere else, more soup and bread, once a man was underground, the Germans had no intention of allowing him to leave the mines, owing to the difficulty in obtaining labour. They could of course force the Poles and those fit enough, if any, from their concentration camps to go down, but not theoretically POW's who were protected under the Geneva Convention and could only volunteer for this work. I decided to volunteer for work, hoping that the working-party was really that which it was purported to be.

I was lucky. I volunteered together with about 200 other POW's, none of whom I knew. We were truthfully told we were needed for work on a German flying field, where they trained German pilots. At first, we were alarmed that this would constitute war work, but we were assured by the Germans that it was not in contravention of the Geneva Convention for the work would be only digging drains, or sewers, and tidying up the area, together with sundry jobs. So, we accepted. With a Sgt in command, we were paraded, counted and checked out of the camp.

From Lamsdorf Station, we were placed in cattle-trucks not too crowded this time and after a few hours including the inevitable shunting process, we detrained at a station and marched to the aerodrome. This was a small training establishment set in a large flat open space, surrounded in the distance by the pine tree woods. The Luftwaffe personnel were accommodated in good well-built wooden barracks. There were two or three hangars, to house the old-fashioned bi-planes that were used for training. It was a grass field without any runway, just the usual windsock flying from a tall mast. Our billet was off this field about a mile or so away, where we were quartered in an old barn, which had a sandy reddish, earth floor with the usual two-tier bunks and the customary wooden tables and forms.

Our food consisted of a Dixie (which was like a small

saucepan) nearly full of soup, thicker, with vegetables, sometimes a hint of meat morsels, which we received at our mid-day break. The same or a varied soup was served on our completion of work and return to camp. We were also given a bread ration double the Lamsdorf issue but no increase in margarine or jam.

We marched to work every day and at this early stage in the war, the Germans had plenty of guards to send on each working party. Later of course this would drastically change. As I had never done any manual work before and was weak, I soon found the extra food did not compensate me for the work I attempted.

The Luftwaffe were all young and fit men, looking very smart in their blue uniforms. Some of them spoke a little English and at that time they were the elite of the German forces, more intelligent than the guards, given officer rank on completion of their training. We used to watch the little planes taking off, swooping, banking and landing. That gave us an interest to break the monotony of the work. One of the pilots was friendly towards me and would exchange some words in English with me as I was working. The guard standing near us would remain discreetly at a short distance, while I was engaged in conversation, which came as a welcome break from pick and shovel. The pilot would stand in front of me looking very smart in characteristic pose that the Fuhrer had once adopted, putting the right hand across the chest inside the tunic, with the thumb exposed. At that time and for long after virtually every German uniformed person adopted this stance, until their regard for the idiosyncratic posture of their beloved ex-corporal, began to wear thin.

The most over rated German word used to POW's was Los! Los! Los! (get on with it) repeated over and over again by the guards attempting to extract the maximum amount of work from us. The German pilot would approach us stealthily and whisper chidingly, Los! Los! Los! I had to laugh for he had a sense of humour most uncommon for a German. I also told the Luftwaffe airman that I was very hungry and inadequately fed. This he complained about to his superiors, who were naturally annoyed, and I was informed by the Sgt. in charge that the Germans considered the ration given to us for this work, sufficient under the Geneva Convention. In view of this, although not in agreement with that report, I decided to lie low and keep quiet. Another good rule I adopted, was never draw attention to yourself if possible.

One day I was working between the barracks, spreading and raking over the soil, when from an open window, a voice called to me. "Are you English?"

I looked across, and saw standing at the window a young Luftwaffe airman of about my age.

I answered, "Yes, I am"

"Come over here", ordered the lad in a pleasant tone.

I did so, and looking into his room which appeared quite comfortable under service conditions, my eyes riveted on a substantial fruit cake resting on a shelf. The airman caught my glance.

"Oh, it is my birthday today, would you like some cake". "Yes please," I said.

He cut me a fair portion, which I took, offered me a cigarette, which I accepted gladly. I wished him a happy birthday and asked him if he flew the biplanes on the field. He became very enthusiastic and said. "Yes, and soon I fly to England".

"What a pity, you won't come back".

The lad laughed and gave me a couple more cigarettes which I of course took, then he wished me goodbye.

When these trainee flyers were on fatigue duties they dressed in black overalls with a black forage cap, trimmed in white braid, and wore black boots like customary German Stiefel.

Sometimes they carried implements, such as shovels or pick-axes as we did, marching along the road, to some kind of special duty. They would be led by the appropriate NCO in command and as was the German custom he would order them to sing by turning his head and calling out.

"Ein, Drie, Vier". One Three Four.

Why this sequence I never knew, nevertheless they would all commence singing the popular songs of the time. Gegen Engeland, was one, which we all learned or other folk songs, such as

Hi Li Hi Lo Hi La Hi Li Hi Lo Hi La Hi Li Hi Lo Hi La Ha Ha Ha Ha.

They would harmonize too and it sounded very good. When we were marching towards them, and we saw them singing along rendering their musical accompaniment, we would spontaneously all commence singing 'Tipperary'.

It's a long way to Tipperary, it's a long way to go. As we neared them we would increase our volume to drown them out, they would do likewise and we would accept this musical challenge with gusto. The NCO in charge of the Luftwaffe squad thought we were paying his singing men a compliment, but we were really "pulling their leg".

In the barn where we lived, the occupant of the bunk opposite mine was a regular Ex India army service little chap, about 27-29 years of age. He was wiry and muscular, and both his arms were tattooed. I secretly called him "Popeye" for he always clenched a virtually empty pipe between his teeth, such was the scarcity of tobacco. He told me he was the British India army boxing champion at his light weight, which I took with a pinch of salt, but he was an entertaining chap to talk to and I quite liked him.

One evening he was seated at the wooden table playing cards with other lads, when an argument developed, following by the usual challenge to fight.

Now in my five years as a POW I will pay tribute to all ranks of prisoners who despite the difficulties, the strain of close living under the conditions of POW life, restrained themselves, reserving their suppressed animosity for our German captors. However, it was inevitable that fights would take place, and I witnessed others. My little friend was matched against a very big, six-foot soldier, and I watched sadly imagining the awful hiding I was sure he would receive. A wide space was cleared as our Sgt in command kept a watchful eye on the proceedings, and the whole barn personnel made up the audience. As the bout, bare fisted of course began, I instantly admired the expertise of my little companion. There was no doubt at all he was a master, but he was getting unfortunately hit, and I could not see him surviving the vigorous onslaught of his heavier opponent. My friend caught a heavy blow and reeled back, staggering. I was afraid it was all over, when he suddenly saw a tunic that had fallen on the floor. The fighter picked it up, dusted it, enquired who owned it and then carefully placed it on one of the forms. He then squared up again to his opponent, for another few exciting minutes. The Sgt in command halted the contest; declared it a draw amid much applause from all of us. When "Popeye" returned to his bunk I warmly congratulated him on his magnificent performance and courage, also speaking of my previous doubt as to his championship ability. He was visibly pleased and whispered to me.

"He was much stronger than I imagined. Did you see me stop, and pick that coat up from the floor? I was out on my feet, but it just gave me a chance to pull myself round to carry on a little bit longer!"

Although my back had now, by mid-September 1940 healed, it was to remain very sensitive if I were bumped or jarred. I was still feeling the pains either side of my groin, whilst marching to and from work. I reported sick and was seen by the Luftwaffe medics, but not a doctor. It was suggested I was probably ruptured, and the Germans decided to return me to Lamsdorf as unsuitable for a working party. Within two days, I was taken together with another POW under escort, marched to the railway station and to my surprise we were allowed to board a fairly comfortable coach. The only other occupants of the coach in the compartment besides us were a Luftwaffe Major and four other

Luftwaffe pilots, all looking remarkably smart. As the train pulled out of the station, I sat next to my companion who was also dressed in a quaint old-fashioned military uniform similar to mine. We were also wearing clogs on our feet. As I started to converse with my friend, I noticed the guard was sitting immediately opposite us, watching us but probably absorbed in his own thoughts. The Luftwaffe Major stood up and leaned over to our compartment, as he did so up sprung the young pilot's heels clicking, so did our guard.

The major addressed me in perfect English.

"So, you are English, come and sit over here".

We all got up and joined his party, the guard sitting at a respectable distance. The Major's educated accent and command of English impressed me, and I complimented him on this.

"But my dear fellow", he replied. "I was educated at Oxford. I was in England for some years."

I pulled out my small tin of tobacco dust, attempting to roll a cigarette, as the major was already smoking when we joined him. "Put that away", remarked the major, pulling out a packet of German cigarettes, and handing both myself and my companion one. Immediately a Luftwaffe airman sprung to his feet, produced a cigarette lighter, and lit our cigarettes. I thought to myself, here we are two scruffy POW in ridiculous clothes, among the elite of the enemy, travelling in style. Who would ever believe me when I tell them? We discussed the war. The major assured me that it would soon be over. England was finished and the Fuhrer would be in Buckingham Palace by Christmas. I had no news

71

of the war, only rumours that despite the Battle of Britain, so far England was undefeated. I began to tell the major in no uncertain terms that we would win, bringing up the sore point of Germany's defeat in the First World War. I think that the Major admired my audacity under the pitiful condition I was in as a POW, for sticking up for Britain. He laughed disagreeing with me and at intervals, he kept plying both of us with cigarettes, the Luftwaffe boys, springing up, lighting first the majors with a bow and then ours. I thoroughly enjoyed this occasion which certainly impressed our guard, for when the major got up to leave the train with his subordinates, he shook my hand and wished me the best of luck. As we left the train later to march to Lamsdorf, the guard eyed me curiously, and I felt well contented.

Return to Lamsdorf – Red Cross parcels arrive

As soon as I was accommodated at Lamsdorf, I was seen by a British medical doctor to whom I imparted the news I was considered ruptured. I had to lower my trousers and the doctor inserted two fingers under my testicles, pushing them hard up the flesh. He looked me straight in the eye and said.

"Ruptured! Balls!"

I laughed, mainly with relief, for I did not want to be incapacitated as a POW. The doctor checked my back and told me if the shrapnel had penetrated a fraction more, I would never have walked again. I considered this escape a miracle, and the second miracle was about to occur. In the barracks where I was given a lower bunk of the three high tier and in which like most POW's we attempted to sleep as much as possible, firstly to relieve the hunger pangs, secondly as a means of escape in dreams.

One day I was seated at the table, when I heard an argument between the Sgt. Major in charge of the hut and a man of about 40 or over years of age. He wore glasses, was a private soldier, and was asking for the foot rags supplied to wrap around the feet. The Sgt. Major refused to give him these saying there were none. I approached the soldier inviting him to sit down. I mentioned that having listened to the discussion, I was sure there were foot rags available, and that in my opinion he was entitled to them. He agreed with me and as we exchanged details, our names and where we lived, he suddenly said excitedly.

"Your father, Maurice Shorrock, tall with curly hair, played the flute in the band at Tidworth. I served with him in 1914-18 War. I was astounded, and found it hard to understand that this man, now a POW in September 1940, should have served with my father. I said to him.

"How could you have been in that war and now in this", for he should have been far too old. He replied with the usual remark. "I only wanted to do my bit, like the rest".

He told me how my father took charge of these young lads, advising them to lead a clean, sober life, he even had a photograph of my father at his home in Sydenham, South-East London.

I considered this so remarkable and for some reason it cheered me up immensely. I was to see him twice more during captivity.

I was considering what next to do. So far, I had received no news from home and I was anxious about my family, especially my mother, as she was unable to walk. From German newspapers that our lads on working parties managed to read, from those who could understand a little German, London was being bombed, and we who came from there were particularly concerned.

About October we received the first Red Cross Issue of a few biscuits per man from a South American Consignment. The whole Stalag was buzzing with rumours of Red Cross Food Parcels, that we would one day receive, and these were so eagerly awaited, that they became the most important topic of conversation.

The colder weather was here, snow was beginning to fall, for Eastern Germany had harsh cold winters and we looked forward with dread to trying to survive, with insufficient food, inadequate heating, no warm clothes. Already some poor lads who had been seriously wounded, or had become very ill had died. They were buried in the graveyard outside the camp.

If I am to give a truthful account as I saw POW life, I must mention one unpleasant subject. As we prisoners were lousy, underfed, shuffling in clogs, it was a great hardship to have to walk the distance to the outside toilets, which everyone did, and had to, if compelled to sit down. Of course, there was great difficulty in finding or obtaining any paper until adequate Red Cross parcels, medical supplies and sundries arrived. Therefore, in order to urinate, many lads used a container, if one were available. Any old can would do, and after use would throw the contents out of the barrack window onto the snow, if the coast was clear. This naturally infuriated the Germans who would send the guards along looking for the culprits, but POW's were wary creatures, and needed some catching. Many POW's who were employed on camp duties, were able to obtain a jam tin, about the size of a pail. These were prized possessions, which the owner could use for carrying extra soup, as a reward for his camp work, or for use to urinate in. A prisoner near me, who was dressed in civilian clothes, a woolen hat, pullover and dark blue trousers, with Wellington boots, had been brought to Lamsdorf from the Channel Islands, which the Germans had annexed in 1940, after the fall of France. They brought him, as other people who were taken off these islands for various reasons, but it was unusual to find someone

75

in civilian clothes in Stalag VIIIB. He was called Big Louis, he was quite tall and looked very miserable, possible because he had no one from the islands to keep him company.

Big Louis had a job in the camp and possessed a jam tin in which he urinated. It was dark and cold in the winter, the barrack lit by a few single bulbs suspended from the ceiling. When Big Louis was at work, I was unable to resist the temptation to use his tin myself. I could not face the walk in the snow, losing the clogs from my feet, trying to keep my feet dry. In using this convenience, I had the added satisfaction of not needing to empty it and I was quite contented with this arrangement.

Unfortunately, as I was in the process, one late afternoon, Big Louis returned unexpectedly, earlier than I had imagined. I was caught red-handed.

"Got you", shouted Louis grabbing my shoulder.

"You are using my tin".

"Sorry Louis", I blurted out. "I just couldn't wait to get to the toilet".

"That's alright", Louis replied. "But if you use it you have to empty it".

I was only too thankful to escape so lightly. So, I agreed, and cautiously began to pick up the jam tin by the handle, noticing it was very full indeed. I should have to be extremely careful in carrying it to the latrines, without spilling any. As I started to make my first step in the long walk Louis stared at me.

"Where do you think you're going" he demanded.

"To the toilet, Louis". I answered.

"Come here, give me that", grumbled Louis.

He took the tin, put it down gently on the floor. His bed was quite near the windows, which had blackout boards, one each side that met in the middle. Louis flung open the shutters, picked up the tin, hurled the contents straight out of the window full into the face of a new guard who had not been completely put in the picture about this very bad habit. Louis, quick as a flash, immediately realising what had happened, slammed shut the wooden frame put his tin far under his bunk, and vanished. I had not seen the guard, but I sensed the terrible urgency, and I quickly made tracks away from that dangerous spot. For a second or two there was silence. Then the most awful blood curdling, inhuman, scream rent the cold night air, enough to scare the living daylights out of me. There was a pounding of feet, and in through the door, burst a raving madman, dripping, soaking wet, with his bayonet in his hand, his rifle in the other and murder in his eyes.

Everyone scattered as he charged, foaming at the mouth, except one young lad who was slow to realise that this German was seeking a victim and had snapped. The Teutonic monster charged at him, but the lad was away in a flash easily outdistancing the guard, by simply disappearing through the washroom into the next barrack, or the next. The German, hot in pursuit raving like a lunatic, did not realise he had lost the race, but the pursued knew perfectly well and as he vanished to safety in the washroom, he paused for a split second, to stick his two fingers up into the air at the German. The guard almost collapsed in a paroxysm of rage, but continued on out of the barrack. After that episode, the Germans threatened to shoot anyone they saw throwing anything out of the window. That did not stop them, only better living conditions would.

That brings me to another incident of a similar nature. Bill was a Geordie, a regular soldier of about 27 years, married with a little boy at home. He was a cheerful character, trying to make the best of a bad lot. I had spoken to him one or twice, and was later to team up with him. At this time, however, during November 1940, he was sitting at a table talking to me and asked if I had any cigarettes. I unfortunately had none for they were extremely scarce. Bill thought for a moment then told me he would have to do something about it. He jumped up on to a table and called out to the whole barrack that he was going to sing for them and hoped they would supply cigarettes if available. I admired his nerve as he started to sing in a pleasing voice, "Little Grey Home in the West". He sang the song right through and when it was ended, received a round of applause. One or two of the lads gave him a few cigarettes. Bill gave me a couple of those and I was impressed by his resourcefulness and kindness.

Later, Bill obtained a job in the camp kitchen, which work was almost impossible to find, unless you had friends employed there. Bill had three other companions so naturally then had to share the extra soup that was available as perks for the job. This combine, as sharing groups were known, also possessed a jam tin, which they used to urinate in. When they were all at work, I used their tin too, which of course they were unaware. Each day one of the group would return at mid-day, carrying the jam tin of soup and store it away from the other tin. At night on the completion of work, they would endeavor to heat the soup by primitive methods, if unsuccessful, they would eat it cold. I used to watch them enviously from my bunk, wishing I had something of that nature to eat. One day, in the gloom of a November afternoon, I crept over to their bunks, seized their tin and urinated. As I put the tin back I realised with horror by the weight, that owing to the dark, I had unfortunately urinated into their soup. I was staggered at the thought of my predicament for I was afraid that if they ate the soup they might be sick, or even poisoned. I lay on my bunk in the cold, deliberating whether to tell them, knowing that if I did, with the importance food had, they would slaughter me. In the end, I decided to confess to Bill, there lie my only hope. I was on tenterhooks until the group arrived back to the barracks. Whilst the others were getting washed, I waylaid Bill and blurted out. "Bill, I'm in terrible trouble, can you possibly help me".

"Whey, lofty lad", said Bill in his Geordie accent.

"Tell me about it".

"Well, Bill", I faltered. "I was using your jam tin this afternoon when you were out and by some awful mistake in the dark, I'm afraid I've peed into your soup". I flinched, fully expecting Bill to punch me in the face. Bill looked at me, put his hand on my shoulder and said.

"Whahy, Lofty Lad, dinna worry, these greedy bastards will eat anything".

79

That night I furtively watched them eating their soup, and saw Bill look over at me and wink. Bill certainly went up in my estimation after that episode.

Mail was now arriving. Almost each day now, the Sgt. Major would suddenly announce.

"Mail up".

Everyone kept perfectly still and quiet, listening hopefully for their name to be called. Each day I saw the lucky recipients collecting their precious letters from their loved ones, but I was disappointed. Then out of the blue, one day I heard my name called. At first, I would not believe it was true, my name was again called. I rushed forward to receive the small regulation white card that POW's and relatives were only allowed to send. The card was from my youngest sister, Doreen, aged nine and the words are engraved upon my memory: -

DEAR LESLIE. I AM WELL, DANNY THE DOG IS WELL. HOPE YOU ARE WELL. LOVE DOREEN.

I could scarcely keep back my tears. Here was the moment for which I had waited so very long, yet, it was everything, but told me nothing about how my family were surviving. It was a long time before I received the welcome news on the longer, white lined letters, that were allowed, two cards, two letters, each per month to send and receive.

In early December, the terrific news circulated the camp. Red Cross Parcels had arrived! Willing volunteers queued up to go to Lamsdorf Station to unload and help bring the parcels into the camp. We were issued one parcel per man. Before I describe the contents, let me first say how much every POW owed to the magnificent work of the Red Cross, and all those engaged in that truly for us, lifesaving work. For as time went on we received clothing, books, games, musical instruments, our whole lives changed and no POW can ever forget the enormous debt of gratitude owed to this marvelous humanitarian organisation. The British parcels varied, containing mostly, a tin of condensed milk, 2oz tea, tin of meat loaf, or bacon or sausages, ¼lb sugar, bar of soap, ½lb tin margarine, raisins, tin of cocoa, biscuits, tin of sardines, ¼lb plain chocolate, and other good things. This parcel contained a fruit cake, which I think was intended for Christmas. With each issue of a parcel, each man received 50 cigarettes in a tin, separately. I am afraid that I, like many others, gorged myself, disposing of my parcel as quickly as possible. It was the most magic day for all of us and one I am sure no early POW will ever forget. The second parcel arrived two or three weeks after Christmas. Now we had something to look forward to and plenty of things to discuss.

In view of the commencement of Red Cross supplies, which incidentally arrived consistently all through captivity, except for breaks of several weeks due to bad weather conditions, when in that case, if the stocks held in the camp were so depleted, one parcel between 2 men, or 3 or 4, was issued. This also applied on every working party. Besides the British parcels, would come to each man a few New Zealand parcels, which were also gratefully received. I personally consider, as did possibly the majority of POW's that the finest Red Cross parcel was the

Canadian. This was a big parcel, and on opening it there would be: -

½ pound of tea, ½ pound of coffee, 5oz bar of milk chocolate, one-pound tin of spam, one-pound tin of skimmed powder milk, ½ pound of prunes, ½ pound of raisins, tin of salmon, tin of sardines, 2 pound of sugar, one pound tin of butter, 12 round thick biscuits.

When you consider one pound of butter per man per week, when the ration in England was 2oz per head per week. Our whole lives revolved around the weekly parcel issue and it was always a moment of eager happy anticipation.

I began to consider events, now we might be able, at the end of 1940, if enough Red Cross parcels arrived, to be able to keep going with the poor insufficient food issued at Lamsdorf. Why then go out to work in the cold bitter weather, when at least you could remain dry in the barrack. Working in the cold sapped your energy and your body demanded more food, which you could not easily obtain. Also in the pipeline was still to come those wonderful personal parcels via the Red Cross, sent with things from your own family. These were allowed one per man every three months. Not everyone got through, but I received lots of these during my five years of captivity. Besides, shoes, socks, underclothes, a blanket as I built up my supply, I used to request, just a shirt and some socks, the remainder of the parcel in bars and bars of chocolate.

I was not the only POW who desired to remain in Lamsdorf, or attempt to do so, there were many others. Just as there were plenty of men eager to get outside the camp not only for a change of scenery, but also for the chance to escape and those who wished to work to keep their mind occupied. Just about this time, of the deep winter snow in January 1941, a German Unteroffizer (Subordinate Officer), with three or four guards entered our barrack with heavy laden sacks, which they proceeded to empty on to the floor. We saw to our amazement heaps of long boots; Stiefels, Polish boots; some British army boots. They grinned at us and told us to help ourselves. I quickly found a suitable pair, and discarded my cumbersome clogs, as did all the other lucky POW's. Somehow, I felt suspicious, so although I put on the boots, I pulled my trousers short as they were, over the top. That of course could not hide them from view. The Germans looked at all of us approvingly and told us to wait there and departed. I vanished into my dark corner, bottom bunk, pulling my blanket over me covering up my boots. The other lads were all comparing their boots, but also suspicious, and keeping a look-out at the windows for the return of the Germans. There was a cry from the observers and everyone could see the Germans carrying lots of long-handled shovels heading towards the barrack. In a flash, everyone vanished as I peered, although carefully hidden to see what ensued. The Germans entered the now empty barrack, cursed, threw down their shovels and ran out of the barrack searching vainly for anyone wearing long black boots. They saw only shuffling POW's in clogs. Apparently, they needed labour to clear the snow from a very near-by aerodrome, hence the ploy with the boots. I was quite pleased and laid low for a while.

German classes - On to the river at Karlsthal

The Germans had advertised within the camp they were starting German language lessons, using part of a spare barrack for this purpose. I reasoned that if they wanted us to learn their language, it was probably to convince us what a wonderful race they were also to encourage us to see their point of view. My sole reason for enrolling as did many others, was to avoid working for them and to stick it out in Lamsdorf if possible. So, we all sat in a classroom atmosphere, listening to a young scholarly German attempt to get us to learn his mother tongue.

To give him his due, our instructor was a quiet refined type, very polite and I did enjoy being with all my friends, as they all became, in the class. We absorbed easy German words which I clearly remember.

"Du bist nicht zu alt genug"

"Du bist nicht zu jung"

We also sang together German Folk songs such as "Rosslein auf der heide" or "Die blauen dragooner sie reiten".

As January and February passed in this fashion, further Red Cross supplies arrived and at long last I was able to procure battledress uniform and underclothes. We were however still waging a relentless war on the lice that plagued us so much and their demise was surely but inevitably destined as soon as we received adequate clothing, better food, more facilities for washing in hot water, all these would gradually occur.

In March 1941, the Germans for reasons we never knew decided to close down the German class and dispatch all of us out on a working party. Perhaps they suspected we were all skiving, or possibly the poor response to these lessons determined their action. The one good thing was that we were all acquainted, in fact I am very sure all good friends and so this working party as regards comradeship, was one of the best I ever knew. I am not sure of the exact number of men, but it must have been near the 100 mark.

We were marched out to Lamsdorf Station, boarded the usual cattle-truck, with our belongings, if any and proceeded to a picturesque village in Dracula country, named Karlsthal. As we left the nearest railway station at Wurbenthal, we then boarded the little railway train travelling in coaches, towards the small station at Karlsthal. The train travelled on a single line high up the steep slopes covered with pine trees. Soon we could see the small winding stream that ran through the village. From our vantage point as we approached, we saw the church with pinnacles such as Turkish or Far Eastern buildings have. We alighted from the train on reaching our destination and marched along the one and only road, crossing the old-fashioned bridge spanning the river, into the village. There were a number of old country houses roughly built and we passed these until we reached a Gasthaus (Inn). This establishment was quite large for such a small village, having a few rooms, let in peacetime holiday seasons.

It boasted a small dance-hall with a stage and at the rear high up were the small windows for the cinema projectionist. There was also a small swimming pool, at the back, now closed and boarded for the duration of the war. A small barbed wire compound had been erected at the side and back, enclosing the dance-hall. Beyond this stretched a half a mile of grass and stony ground, leading to the bank of the river which flowed through the village and passed about fifty yards from the rear of the Gasthaus.

We were allotted the dance-hall as our living quarters and in them were new two-tiered bunks with straw palliasses for our beds. There were enough windows on one side of this room, double-glazed, with the usual black out wooden shutters, to give us plenty of daylight. We were quite satisfied with this accommodation and began to choose our beds, unload our possessions and settle in. In charge of our working party there was an Unteroffizier, plus six guards.

Our job was to widen the river, a tributary of the River Neisse, which flooded in winter causing discomfort to the villagers. In the middle of the river at its widest point, clearly visible from our compound, was a huge island of stony rubble, that had to be first cleared, then the river surface, straightened, deepened, and the banks built up by fascines. These were six feet long bundles of branches intertwined and bound, placed all along the bank and then rubble tipped over them, raked smoothly over to increase the height of the river banks. From our compound to the left we could see the very high slope of green, upon which were the graves of former villagers. At night, even in wartime so far and remote was this place, that tiny little lights were suspended from each grave, clearly visible with the naked eye. These were put there to scare away the vampires! The sleepy village was surrounded by these high almost, very small mountains of pine trees. Above the river winding along the side of the hill was the single railway line hidden by the pines. There were two trains a day in each direction, from which we could accurately denote the time. The only great disadvantage was the long working hours 7.00 am to 6.00 pm, summertime, shorter in winter, then the work nearly all snow-clearing. Also, the guards were very unpleasant and we found their constant harrying us to work hard, tedious, and greatly annoying. At the moment, we were taking stock of our surroundings, enjoying the quietness, together with the pleasant scenery as opposed to the grim discomfort of Lamsdorf. We commenced work on our new river job, escorted by three guards, leaving behind our small camp staff and any sick, under the control of our NCO, Sgt. Les Parry. We were given shovels and picks; wheelbarrows were also available together with wooden trestles. The Germans also provided us with several pairs of Wellingtons for the use of those compelled to work in the shallow water of the stream. Most of these boots were not entirely waterproof, and our feet were cold and damp, in the early spring weather. Planks of wood were laid, end to end across the ground and on trestles over water, to enable wheelbarrows laden with rubble to be carted to fresh positions.

The work was hard and the days very long, also in the beginning the guards would harry us as often as possible with their endless calls of "Los! Los! Los!" It would take months to condition them, until the monotony of constantly walking up and down lines of men apparently working hard, caused them to relax. We became grateful towards anyone who could give us a break, by diverting the attention of the guards or causing them to laugh. Here we found Ernie indispensable. Ernie was older than most of us possibly 30-35 years of age, a man of medium height, he was a natural comedian, soon causing the guards to laugh at his antics. He acted as though he was slightly mad, performing gestures of pantomime with comments in gibberish. The guards loved it and as they paced up and down, chatting to each other, glancing occasionally towards us, whereupon Ernie would prance up and down, waving his arms, and entertaining them. Now Ernie Marshall was the raker. He had a long handled rake and as we all trundled our wheelbarrows along the boards and tipped them in front of Ernie, he would busily ply his rake smoothing the earth and stones to build up the river banks. What the guards did not know was that Ernie was indicating each time to us, so that we could wheel our virtually empty barrows, along the plankboard run and tip them away from the side where the guards were standing. If they approached too close, as they often did, we would fill the barrows fairly full and then make a legitimate run. I quite enjoyed the thrill of wheeling these empty barrows up and down day after day. It was not so tiring as full loads.

Every so often, a nasty looking civilian overseer would arrive with his Theodolite. This he would set, peer through the eye-glass, surveying and measuring the work progress. His first sight would cause him to frown with impatience and he would take another reading then another. Meanwhile, we would dutifully push our loaded barrows conscientiously up and down. Suddenly we would hear a bellow of rage, then the overseer would rush up to the guards and accuse them of allowing us to laze about. The guards would treat him with scorn telling him he did not know what he was doing and soon to our delight, a ding-dong row would take place everyone shouting and screaming at each other. We thoroughly enjoyed all this and after the departure of the overseer, Ernie would tell the guards he was mad, but not as mad as himself. This would restore the humour of these morons, and we would carry on.

There were many other ways we could slow down the work. We could with a deft movement of the foot cause the planks to fall off the trestles, barrows would topple over, everyone getting in each other's way, until at last order was restored. Another ruse was to pick on an "easy guard" for guards were often changed. Then with our smattering of German, chat to him, enquiring about his family, any children and so forth. Out would come photographs which we would pass around so that everyone had a good rest, leaning on their shovels. We also went frequently to the box-like wooden toilet where one could relax, but not too long, for the guard would kick the door, shouting "Raus! Raus!".

As the weeks passed, conditions improved with Red Cross parcels issued each week. Adequate supplies of clothing, English soap, a chance once a week to get hot water to wash ourselves and clothes. We began to win the battle against lice, which we ultimately did. I was sharing my Red Cross parcel with Bill Telford in a partnership of dividing equally all we had. This was the method everyone used in parties of two, three, four or even more. At Karlsthal I had a fine set of comrades, every man was my friend, and I am sure they regarded me as theirs. We had nearly all been in the German class at Lamsdorf, so we knew one another quite well.

Les Parry did a first class job at keeping us in order, and being a regimental boxer, we knew what to expect if we went to extremes. Les did not need to resort to that because we all behaved in my opinion in a decent manner, directing our animosity only towards our captors. We acquired a gramophone with a few English records from the Red Cross, and I can hear it now, just as then, each morning early. Les Parry would invariably put on a record of Denny Denys, the English Bing Crosby singing "Riding Home", or Jessie Matthews singing "Gang Way". These two tunes would rouse us to start another long day out on the little river.

One day I was working in the river standing in shallow water, shoveling rubble from the river bed, when I noticed a lad using a wooden mallet to knock stakes into a fascine. Three or four long stakes had to be driven through the fascine (bundle of sticks and leaves, etc.) at even spaces to anchor this to the river bed. I noticed the lad was only gingerly tapping the stake which required a heavier blow. The guard was yelling to him to hit the stake harder. It was obviously so easy to do, that I waded across to show him how. I took the mallet from his eager grasp, raised it high to bring it down heavily on the stake, noticing the guard nodding with approval at my effort. I at once realised by the sound of the dull thud, that previous blows had hit the stakes with the handle of the mallet causing it to split. As I struck the stake again, off flew the mallet head, just missing the guard on the bank, who was standing too close.

"Sabotage. Sabotage" yelled the guard furiously and ordered me to go and get another mallet from the shed. When I returned I passed the instrument to my friend to use, which he accepted reluctantly. After a couple of blows, I heard again the ominous crack as the handle hit the stake splitting a good way down. It was my turn now, so I carefully manipulated the mallet, hoping the head would remain intact but knowing full well it would not. As the guard shouted to me to hit it hard, I did, and off flew the head again. The guard cursed and shouted, going into his act and I could only kick myself for having got myself into this predicament. The other lad was told to obtain a new mallet. On his return, I decided to seek refuge in the wooden toilet which thankfully the guard did not raise much objection to.

When I emerged after staying there as long as possible, I quickly pretended another guard was calling to me for assistance and so got away. There was always fun and drama at work. I was in line with several others digging away at a drainage ditch, when the river expert headed our way, with a very big, ugly guard. The expert was called Weber. He was a little old man, goodness knows how ancient he was, he had a white beard, wore a peak cap, blue jacket, grey trousers tucked into his Wellington boots. He possessed a prized object in wartime Germany, a spirit level.

All along the bank were small pegs joined together with string which he had laboriously marked out as part of some reclamation plan he was following. He pointed to me and the guard ordered me to assist Weber, in whatever he needed doing, leaving us to join his crony further along the bank. Beaming at Weber, I jumped out of the ditch, seized his wrinkled old hand, and shook it in a warm welcome. The old man turned away, beckoning me to follow and I knew the lads expected something from me to break the monotony. I bent down and starting pulling up the pegs attached to the string, one after the other. Weber turned round, saw me and shouted.

"Nein, Nein, Nein,"

I smiled happily at him, and seizing a hammer that was lying on the ground nearby, started to knock the stakes into the ground, so that they virtually disappeared. Weber came trotting up babbling away in fast German, so I took his spirit level from him and marched off quickly towards a workbench, where I knew there was a saw.

Weber plodded pathetically after me, but I got there first, grabbed the saw and started to pretend to saw his spirit level in half. I made the first slight nick in the wood, knowing these were unobtainable in Germany. Weber screamed as he thought I would saw it in half. The guard came running up, the ugly one, and started shouting at me. First, he called me a big ape, that was strictly incorrect and completely the reverse. He called me an idiot, besides other selected names. His mate came up and I heard them say they were going to punish me. They told me I was being put back on the wheelbarrow run. This of course was an ideal job as I have previously mentioned, but at once I wrung my hands in anguish, looking very upset, and begging them not to. They both roared with delight, almost hugging each other with glee as I moaned away. Thoroughly pleased with themselves, they pushed me, not unkindly towards the wheelbarrows. I knew the lads were enjoying the farce, so I played it out to the full, reluctantly taking my shovel, sighing as I proceeded to fill the barrow, only until they left me, crowing with delight.

Incidents of this nature gave us immense satisfaction putting one over on them at every possible opportunity. To describe the next occurrence, I must explain that some sensible soldiers on being captured were smart enough to promote themselves to either Sgt, with three stripes, or Corporal or bombardier, two stripes. Now if the Germans accepted these men as bona fide NCO's under the Geneva Convention, they could not be forced to work, as private soldiers were, but were allowed to volunteer. Usually if the working party was of reasonable size, the Sgt could command, assisted by an NCO. These men were called "Stalag Corporals", and there were very many of them. I became one towards the end as you will hear. Often the Germans would send genuine or Stalag Corporals out to work however much they protested.

Johnny was a big man. He was a corporal, because he sported the two stripes. He decided that he would not work anymore for the Germans and considered he should be returned to Lamsdorf under the protection of his rank. So he informed Les Parry, who was in charge, that he would not work the following day. I think everyone was alarmed because we all knew how the Germans reacted to obstinacy. The next morning, as we paraded outside in the little compound, Johnny remained inside, refusing to come out. The guards rushed at the door and in their haste to get at Johnny, someone, bless him, tripped up a horrible little guard named Schneider, who cut his knee. Schneider cursed and swore and proceeded to the pump in our yard to soothe his knee, forgetting his part in the episode. The other three guards rushed in and started hitting Johnny with their rifles, as Johnny stood there, a very brave man. Les quickly summoned the Unteroffizier in charge, who stopped the guards, ordered them to take the rest of us to work and as we anxiously left the compound, we were concerned about Johnny.

I remember the day so well, for as we were working as slowly as possible, we saw Johnny reluctantly approaching our site, being escorted by a guard. Evidently Les Parry had prevailed upon him to go out to avoid further trouble for himself. Johnny reached us and picked up his shovel attempting to shovel the earth and rubble into a heap to be cleared. The guard stood close to him, shouting at him continually, exhorting him to work harder. I was watching this scene closely, wondering how long Johnny would endure this treatment. Suddenly he threw down his shovel on the ground and refused to work. Before the guard could do anything the Unteroffizier had approached unobserved and now appeared on top of the river bank. We waited anxiously, the guard hesitating too, the German NCO strode down the bank, took his revolver from his holster, walked right up to Johnny, pushing the barrel into his chest, saying quite firmly.

"Arbeit oder nicht" - Work or Not.

Johnny stood straight as a pole, looked down at the Unteroffizier, who was much smaller, eyeball to eyeball, and replied quite firmly.

"Nicht arbeit"

There was complete silence as everyone had stopped work and we watched with bated breath, our eyes glued on these two figures.

"Arbeit oder nicht"

"Nicht arbeit" said Johnny.

I could not believe what I was seeing, for the German was a grim silent man with a good deal of menace in his manner. Seconds passed, until the Unteroffizier withdrew his gun and ordered the guard to take Johnny back to our lager. The Unteroffizier strode away, as the guard screaming at Johnny to move, unslung his rifle, pushing Johnny in the back. I watched them as slowly moving along, Johnny would stop, the guard shouting, would rattle the bolt of the rifle jabbing him in the back. This was repeated time and again, over and over, until the two figures disappeared from sight. I have never seen such magnificent bravery for Johnny could have easily lost his life for such defiance. After work had finished and we returned to our lager, Johnny was stating that he would not go out the next day. We all thought the world of him, but added our arguments and persuasion to that of Les, pointing out that the Germans would not recognise his rank and would force him to work. I know that Johnny also had our interests at heart, when he very reluctantly, but very wisely, agreed to carry on working. No one, not even the Germans could doubt the courage and obstinacy of this man.

Doing as little as possible - The first sugar beet detail

We had to make our own entertainment in the evenings after our bowl of soup had been eaten and our utensils washed under the one pump, outside in our tiny compound. The Germans paid us camp money at various intervals, called Lagergeld. With this at first, we were able to buy razor blades, some form of toothpaste, a little writing material, even bottles of mild lemonade, occasionally, but these items in war-time Germany soon were exhausted, so we pooled our money in order to purchase musical instruments. Bill who was my partner, obtained a trumpet, Danny, a clarinet, Bob, a violin, Tanky, our versatile Scots lad, a piano accordion. We also had a guitar, Charlie Crisp, a curly haired lad, had a mouth-organ, and someone else a banjo mandolin.

Tanky was so called for he was in the Tank Corps, was our musical inspiration, and suggested we try and form a small band. Now this was really music to my ears for I always liked music, but unfortunately, I had never learnt that art, but I enjoyed trying to play tunes on the Banjo Mandolin after Tanky had shown me the basic idea. I also used to borrow a guitar, for not one of us could play, so I tried to pick out a tune unsuccessfully, but Tanky noticed my attempts. To my surprise and enjoyment, the band were making sense to us, starved of any kind of music for almost a year. Tanky suggested that I could join the band, with the borrowed guitar, and he taught me the three chords he knew, which were C, D7 and G. He showed me that by strumming these chords, it would give a sense of rhythm to the band. I could not believe that such a poor musical accompaniment could be of any use, but everyone was so enthusiastic that I was delighted to have the honour to be included. We played everything by ear and memory that we could, and I loved it, and so I am sure did everyone else, judging by the warm appreciation our efforts evoked. I was amazed that such talent existed among so few in numbers. Even the guards would listen to our renderings, for they had nothing to amuse them after the day was over.

These were really happy days for me and I am sure my comrades, for so many of them gave turns, tried to sing, acted in plays, and of course the irrepressible Ernie would give us hilarious performances. We also acquired a proper table tennis outfit complete with trestles and I have a feeling that this was made by the lads out of materials provided by the Germans. We were receiving via Lamsdorf, through the Red Cross, various games, boxing gloves, besides reserves of clothing and of course the lifesaving Red Cross food parcels.

Pat Howlett, a Lancashire lad, was a special friend of mine, for my father had been born and lived for years in Blackpool. Pat was a very good heavyweight boxer. He had a dry laconic sense of humour that was a good foil to mine and I often worked with Pat, or Harry Alderson, Charlie Crisp, Bob Blezzard, Frank Palser as well as Bill Telford, and many other wonderful chaps. Pat prevailed on me to spar with him and I agreed, after extracting a promise from him that he would only very lightly tap me or better still not at all. Pat laughingly agreed, but in the course of our little "work-out", he forgot himself and gave me a very colourful black eye. I was annoyed but everyone enjoyed my discomfiture so much that even I saw the funny side of it. I was very wary of sparring with Pat after that. After the war, Pat came to my home and stayed for a week's holiday.

Bill, our trumpet player was of course my partner, sharing our food parcels, the same as other teams and combines did. After we were locked inside our dance hall room each night at about nine o'clock in summer and earlier in winter, we had to resort to a make shift toilet, which was on the stage behind a flimsy screen.

Hopefully we need only to urinate during the locked in period, and this was done into a small wooden funnel that protruded through a hole outside the wall into a large kind of rain barrel. This barrel would of course fill within one or two days, and Bill, the most cheerful soul who volunteered to empty it, would be called by a guard, then proceed to the rear of our dance-hall.

He would use an old tin or bucket and fill it from the contents of the barrel, walk over the rough ground for about fifty yards, and empty the container into a drainage pitch. Bill would sing cheerful ditties while performing this vital task for us all and I never gave it any thought.

Bill was unwell for two or three days, so Les Parry asked me if I would empty the barrel in this case. I of course agreed, and the guard collected me and we went to the back of the Gasthaus. The guard pointed to the container, then to the barrel and wandered off quite some yards from me. I thought that a little strange, but perhaps he was moody, so I cheerfully seized the old bucket and advanced towards the barrel. I stopped in my tracks, on getting within a foot, for I was overwhelmed and gripped by the appalling stench of ammonia. I gasped and retreated and again charged the barrel, but before I could dip the bucket in, I was defeated by a desire to be violently sick. I fought against this and by an effort of willpower succeeded in scooping some contents, staggering away to dispose of this in the ditch. I finally managed to complete this awful job, though I am sure I did heave a little in the process. The guard rejoined me and we returned to our respective quarters. I was sadly chastened with the thought of having to perform this necessary task again, but how on earth could Bill do it and cheerfully sing as well. When Bill, fortunately, was very soon able to resume his occupation, I put this to him. He just laughed and replied.

"There's nothing to it, lofty lad. It's a piece of cake."

The weather was fine and warm, I was feeling good, no more problems with walking, that vanished for good, the outdoor exercise, coupled with regular Red Cross food, was improving the health of everyone. Thursday, May 15th 1941, dawned, it was my 21st Birthday. I had shown my friends a postcard I had written to my mother, stating that I promised to return home on my 25th birthday. We all thought this quite a joke, but I will reveal later the irony of this.

After work had finished that day and we were seated at our respective tables in our groups, Les made the announcement that it was my 21st birthday. Amid cheers, he went on to say that he was sure all my comrades would allow me to be first served with the soup that was over. Generally, this soup was issued in strict rotation in complete fairness, table by table. Everyone again applauded, so I collected my extra bowl of soup, thanking them all for the nicest birthday present I had ever received. After things had been cleared away, I was aware of Les and his group whispering together. Suddenly they advanced towards me, Les holding a tin of Cherry Blossom blacking, open, in one hand and a brush in the other. I was seized by several pairs of hands and despite my desperate resistance, my face and neck were thoroughly blacked. There were hoots and yells of laughter, as I realised the intention was to blacken me completely. I struggled with all my might, then, by a stroke of good fortune, roll call was sounded as usual by the guards shouting.

"Apell, apell, eintreten, los, los, los"

This had to be obeyed, so we immediately trooped outside into the little compound, lining up in threes for the count. I was pushed to the front rank and as the Unteroffizier with his second in command took the count, they paused as they reached my black face and I saw faces twitch with amusement. Les explained the charade as they passed on.

On returning to the dance-hall, Charlie Crisp produced his mouth-organ, starting to play the tunes I liked. "Deep Purple", "Over the Rainbow", "Pennies from Heaven". Ray Noble tunes, Cole Porter, Gershwin. I accompanied him on the banjo mandolin and was completely happy. As I looked around at all those noble lads, my friends, I considered myself fortunate to be regarded so very well by them.

The work on the river was proceeding slowly despite all our efforts to slow it down. We had built a wheelbarrow run on trestles across the stream, which in places was about three feet deep. I was pushing my barrow behind Tom, who was Ernie's partner. Tom had been a London bus driver before the war, but at this moment in time, with his empty pipe clenched between his teeth, he did not look safe driving his wheelbarrow. I sensed that Tom would fall, he was wavering precariously. I put down my wheelbarrow on the plank, and held it, to steady myself when like a slow moving picture, Tom fell sideways, with his barrow, into the stream. Everyone including the guards roared with laughter, as Tom emerged, the water streaming down his face, with his pipe still firmly in his mouth. He clambered out soaking wet. The guards took him into the small hut, where we used to eat our lunch, so that he could dry out. The German humour was apparent if you had a misfortune. If someone could break a leg, this would put the guards in a pleasant mood all day. I once slipped during the winter up to my thighs in the icy water. The guards roared with delight, taking me into the hut round a hot stove to dry out, giving me as much time as I needed. We would always use mishaps, genuine or affected, to extract the maximum advantage of avoiding work.

On 22nd June 1941, the Germans attacked Russia, intending with their Blitzkrieg tactics to finish them off in a few weeks. Many of my friends thought this would happen, but I had my doubts, for I had read of Napoleon's retreat from Moscow and knew of the vastness of that country. I had to admit, however, that so far in this war, everything had gone wrong for us.

When the weather became colder towards the winter, work on the river had to slow down, especially during snow, which came in October and remained until March. It used to get extremely cold with icicles hanging from the pine trees, even waterfalls flowing down the hillsides froze. Snow clearing was our principal winter occupation but first we had a taste of the sugar beet operation.

We had to pack all our belongings and march to the railway station, where we boarded cattle-trucks bound for a tiny place called Wazzerowitz. Here out in the wilds was a sugar beet factory surrounded by many fields of sugar beet crop. It was a small factory designed to refine sugar from the beet, and there were many of these in this part of the Third Reich. All around the factory was a 20 foot deep concrete circle, at the bottom of which was a yard wide channel that disappeared into the factory itself. Covering the channel were sheets of iron plate divided into three feet sections, the last few feet that entered the plant being uncovered. The sugar beet would be dug out of the fields by civilians, mainly Poles or forced labour and driven in mule carts into the factory. The carts unloaded into the covered channel, the beet reaching the top and heaped as high as a pitch fork could throw them.

This was our job and we were provided with special forks, the prongs of which had tiny iron nobs on them, to enable the beet to be gathered up. A fork full of beet was very heavy and tossing one up on a huge pile was hard work. This chore would continue, and go on even when the factory started to process the beet.

Into the channel would be pumped hot water and as each iron plate was removed, a worker at the bottom of the channel would hook down the beet with a metal implement, causing a minor avalanche and a continuous flow of beet into the factory. I was not aware of this process until my next sugar beet season. At this time, I never saw inside the plant, as the Germans had adequate labour forces to operate without our assistance.

It was very difficult working in the icy conditions trying to fork frozen beet, but usually the weather was only generally cold with plenty of snow. The Germans billeted us in barns or any temporary accommodation, for the season only lasted a couple of months. When the last mounds of beet were being shifted, dozens of grey field mice would scurry away from their winter quarters, chased by us all, as a welcome relief to the end of a tedious job.

On our return to Karlsthal, we entered our abode and quickly lit the stove in the middle of the floor, feeding the flames with spare pieces of wood we always collected and stored. It was not yet dark and as we stored our belongings on our various beds, we all began itching rather badly. Soon we were unable to obtain a moment's respite from this affliction, then, as the lights were switched on by the guards, from their quarters, I saw a sight that the reader will find hard to credit. Across the whole of the floor was an undulating mass of millions of red fleas, the floor looked as if it had been painted red. During our two months absence, they had invaded and multiplied nesting in the straw of our beds. Apparently, this was a common phenomena in this part of Sudetenland, being plagued by those little red devils. None of us slept that night, most of us sitting up. The next day, we took out all the straw and burnt it, being provided with fresh straw in replacement. Now we thoroughly scrubbed out our bed bunks and the hall, thoroughly washed and changed our clothing. That dealt a mortal blow to the fleas, from which they never recovered.

Christmas 1941, was celebrated as best we could, exchanging gifts wherever possible, using our Red Cross Parcels to provide our meal. The band played, the lads sang as we all remembered our loved ones and as usual optimistically looked forward to returning home by the Christmas of 1942. Of course, I must recall here the tremendous news of 7th December 1941, with the attack by the Japanese on Pearl Harbour, bringing the Americans into the war. We were now not alone, for we had two further allies. We at last felt that the war must now turn in our favour. Curious rumours always abounded, one of the most consistent was that Turkey had entered the war on our side. Why this should have been looked for I cannot imagine.

As the days slowly passed towards spring our little world was about to be shattered. The Germans informed us about April 1942, that 20 or 30 men were required for a new working party.

Naturally, no one really desired to move from Karlsthal, especially not knowing the job or where we would be going. The Germans selected, and I found myself included. Bill also, Tanky too. Our party numbered about 22. Les Parry was going with us in command. We said goodbye to our friends who were remaining, and off we marched to the station to board our train. I think that as our party was so small, we travelled by carriage and not cattle truck. Accompanying us was a Gefreiter (Corporal), in charge and three guards.

I do not recall the name of the place where we worked, but I remember we were billeted in a barn with the usual two-tiered bunks. From this place it was quite a long march to our work area and when we reached it, we found a grassy meadow, with a stream on one side with clear water, not very deep, and on the other side we had to dig a channel about six feet deep, by about 12 feet wide that was to run for some considerable distance. After the top soil was removed, we found layers of yellow slate interspersed with blue clay. It was hard, slogging pick and shovel work and as we worked two or three abreast, in close proximity, we were under observation from the guard, one I think on duty each day. Consequently there was no opportunity to skive, or to arrange mishaps, or divert attention.

It was going to be a short stay for me, only a matter of weeks. Les Parry, came and saw me after work one evening and told me the Germans required the transfer of three men from the working party. He said that my selection was entirely at his discretion, because he felt that the work was too hard for me to perform. As to my fear of being sent to the mines, he assured me that from what he had heard there was no danger of that. I recognised the inevitable; at heart, I was not too sorry to leave that party, it was too small with very few opportunities to avoid work. My regret at leaving Bill who had been a good friend and partner was genuine and sad. Also I was again leaving the last members of the Karlsthal party.

The three of us were taken by one guard and we boarded a lorry for the nearest railway station was in the town of Troppau. From there we travelled on a train in comfort, not a very long journey and arrived at a new place named

Branddorf. This was situated in a pleasant area, high up, with a view of the surrounding forests of pines. On the site were three wooden type bungalows each containing one large room with several two-tier bunks. The full complement was about 100 POW's mainly New Zealand men who had been captured on Crete, and Australians taken prisoner in North Africa.

Our job was to dig foundations and assist in the unloading of timber, used in the construction of several of these bungalows, probably intended as a civilian camp. I soon settled in, now on my own, without anyone to share with, as I knew nobody on that working party. They were a good bunch of lads, and I found the work a great deal easier, with more opportunities to avoid doing too much hard graft. It was the spring of 1942. Already I had nearly completed two years of captivity yet there was nothing to suggest that the war would end for a very long time.

I found the New Zealanders had a very high regard for the British, which was entirely reciprocated and I got on well with the Aussies, once you got to know them. I, as all the other Britons, used to gently chide the Aussies. We would say to them. "Can one really see the marks on your legs, where you were chained to the Hulks".

This always got them going. Or we would tease them.

"We appreciate you coming 12,000 miles, half-way around the world to assist us in this war, but really we could have managed on our own."

The Aussies would snarl back.

"Strewth, you jokers were kicked out of every place you went, the B.E.F. BACK EVERY FRIDAY".

Our reply was

"Yes, I know, but we were only fooling the Germans into believing they were winning."

The Aussies would explode.

"Winning! They were. You were bloody well losing all the time, till we came and helped you".

Now we knew they had been captured by the Italians or "Eyeties" as everyone called them. Everybody despised the Eyeties. We would say to the German guards, picking our man out carefully. "The Germans are doing very well in the war. Is it because the Italians are helping you?"

The guard would spit on the ground in contempt, and let loose a string of curses on the luckless Italians. This always worked, as it did when we would lead the Aussies on about their exploits in the desert war. After they had coloured their deeds, we would innocently say.

"Who captured you then, was it the Germans".

The Aussies would look uncomfortable and reply.

"No, the EYETIES".

We would raise our eyebrows.

"You were captured by the Eyeties. We were captured by the Germans!"

We would emphasise this to show the distinction in being taken prisoner by the better army. It was all good fun, and helped to pass the long weary day, on the site.

As time went on we began to get fed up with Bransdorf. Red Cross Food Parcels were delayed, and we missed several weeks issue. This was a serious blow to us, for the German food ration was insufficient. We had a very efficient small Scots Sgt. in charge of our party, and though he did his utmost we were unable to improve conditions. Consequently, the Aussies and New Zealanders who outnumbered us, after discussion decided that we should all go on strike. I could not believe my ears and enquired what they thought a strike was. They told me that they would barricade the doors overnight with the forms and tables and refuse to turn out for work the next day. I had grave misgivings in view of the German temperament in the middle of a total war, their reaction on being informed we were going to defy them and refuse to work. Moreover, as the Germans were not too particular in abiding to the Geneva Convention, what provision had that agreement made for a situation like this.

It was all agreed and as we turned in that night, with the flimsy doors locked as always by the guards, I awaited with trepidation the coming of the dawn.

The 'Crested Eagle' that Les observed sinking at
Dunkirk.

Les (middle) with Kenny Russel (left) and another friend at Campshill Road, in Lewisham, London. *c.*1939 The picture was colourised by myself.

Les' Uncle, 2nd Lt Thomas Dudley Ralph Shorrock, killed in the battle of the Menin Road Ridge on 20th September 1917.

Dorothy Bryan (Right), Les' Mother and his Grandmother,
Florence Bryan. *c.*1898

Dorothy Bryan, Les' Mother. *c.* 1910

Les' Sister Doreen (left) with her older Sister Madge.

*c.*1939

Les' Great Aunt Helen who was killed by a V2 rocket. She
is pictured here with her beloved Danny the dog.

Les' Father, Maurice and Les' Sister, Doreen at
Dymchurch. *c.* 1935

Les' Mother aged 52. *c.*1946

Les (back row, second from left) at Lamsdorf, Stalag
VIIIB. This may have been on one of the working parties.
*c.*1941

Les in his uniform at home *c.*1939

Les with Gladys, whom he married on 4th August 1947.
Photo colourised by Marina Amaral.

Les Married Gladys (My Grandmother) on 4th August 1947
in Forest Hill, South East London.

Left to right: Babs (Les' Sister), Dudley (Les' Brother),
Gladys, Irene (Gladys' Sister).

Les, Gladys and their daughter Pauline (My mother) on
the Isle of Wight. *c.*1959

Les at the beach *c*.1950

Les receiving an award from a director of Truman's Brewery for a poetry competition, in which Les came first place. *c*.1980

Les on holiday in Weymouth. *c.*1970

Me with my Grandad Les in Plumstead Gardens. *c.*1979

Les at The Cutty Sark in Greenwich, South East London
c.1986

Harry Alderson who is mentioned in the chapter 'On Strike – The second sugar beet experience'

Harry Alderson in the middle, front row.

A picture from Stalag VIIIB. Les in 2ⁿᵈ row from the back, fourth from the left.

Harry Alderson is Front Row, far right.

Les, taken from the picture on the previous page.

Les, at home. *c.*1990

On strike! - The second sugar beet experience - Booted out!

We all arose the next day getting ready as usual as if we were going to work, but instead barricaded the door of our hut, as did the boys in the other two huts. All too soon there came the shouts of the German guards ordering us out to work, as they came across to unpadlock each door. Not a soul moved or emerged from their huts. The guards kicked the door and pushed to get in, but as the lads were all putting their weight behind the barricades, there was no chance of that. The lads were also calling out in German.

"Nicht Arbeit". Besides insults and taunts.

The guards ran across the compound to their quarters to inform the Unteroffizier that he had a mutiny on his hands. I crowded round the windows, together with many others to watch events, and what I saw did not inspire me with very much confidence. The German NCO emerged, with his steel helmet on, and paraded all the guards, those off-duty, or who had been asleep as well. One can imagine their feelings. We heard the guttural commands to put on steel helmets, fix bayonets, the Unteroffizier drew his revolver and in his other hand held a bayonet. When they were ready the Unteroffizier led the way, followed by the grim determined guards.

Fortunately, they chose the third but which was on their left and possibly decided to attack left to right. They reached the door kicking, and hitting it with their rifle butts. The door collapsed and they swiftly threw aside the flimsy barricade. Next, we heard yells, cries and oaths coming from our comrades' quarters. Suddenly they tumbled out into the compound getting hit as they emerged. One lad was bayonetted in the thigh fortunately not seriously. The next but received the same treatment, and their occupants shouting and swearing emerged. Now it would be our turn. I was lying on the bottom bunk with a New Zealander above me, a ginger-haired lad who was called "Bluey".

As the Unteroffizier crashed inside our hut, "Bluey" was hurling insults at the Germans. The NCO rushed at Bluey and brought his bayonet down but Bluey avoided that by a lightning movement, the blade crashed on his wooden bed removing a chunk of wood. Now I do not know to this day who went through the door first, whether Bluey preceded me, or I him, I was only thankful to find myself out there all in one piece. There was a period of pandemonium with all the Germans yelling, kicking and swiping, but eventually having achieved a remarkable victory over unarmed men, the Germans calmed down. We were all marched out to work and once there we soon realised the humour of the situation, but to me, I never heard of another strike by POW's in all my years of captivity.

The Red Cross parcels were delivered and at last we received a regular supply again, which made all the difference in enduring captivity.

The summer months passed without any further incidents and on the approach of October 1942, we were all told to get ready to move to a sugar beet plant near Troppau. We duly packed our belongings not realising that we would never again return to Bransdorf, which would not have bothered us in any case. We made our usual cattle truck journey, which fortunately was not of long duration and eventually arrived at a large factory, much bigger than the first one I had worked at. When we were settled in our billet, the usual arrangement of two-tiered wooden bunks with the customary straw mattress, we visited the many other POW, who were housed in a large brick building, probably one of the factory buildings now not normally used. To my delight I found that the old Karsthal work force with all my friends, except of course Bill and the others, were being employed there. We were all so pleased to be able to exchange details and relate all our news. Although I was officially with the ex-Bransdorf party, I managed to work on the sugar beet detail with most of my friends.

One day, a lad asked me if I would like to join him on a good job, where one worked one hour and then received two hours off. Of course, night work was also necessary, on this particular work, but I was prepared to have a go at anything rather than stand out in the open in cold weather, unloading carts full of sugar beet. I was taken to where the sugar beet was hooked down from the mountainous pile all around the factory and shepherded into the warm water channel, which washed and carried the beet into the processing plant. My first hour of work was fairly reasonable, for which, the implement provided consisting of a wooden pole about four feet long to the end of which was attached a metal hook, the beet fell almost of its own momentum. All I had to do was to lift the iron plate, which the cascading beet had uncovered, and simply renew the process.

When darkness fell the working area in the deep concrete ditch was only dimly lit, so the guard had difficulty in seeing me, but knew I was down there presumably working hard for the Fatherland. The sugar beet mountain would become stuck, with beet intertwined, so that hard raking and pulling became necessary. Soon tired of this boring procedure, though it was warmer being enclosed by the sugar beet and protected from the wind by the deepness of the canal. I stopped moving the beet. Naturally from a steady flow into the processing plant the beet trickled to almost a stop, except for a few single floating beets carried away by the canal. Very soon irate voices were heard shouting from the darkness. These soon changed to yells echoed dutifully by the guards, for me to slave away again. To keep them quiet, I gave a few desultory pokes at the huge piles of beet and if they tumbled down, good, if not, hard luck. I knew the end was inevitable but I did not care, for I had lost my enthusiasm for this boring job, even if I possessed any in the first place. I managed to survive for an hour or so, by shouting out various excuses but in the end, I was ordered out of the canal and sent packing to shovel the beet.

Goods wagons full of beet were brought right into the plant by means of railway siding lines. Two men to a goods wagon to unload was considered all that was needed. I was working with a friendly New Zealand chap, and as usual we got the wagon doors open, whereupon a heap of beet obligingly fell onto the ground.

A couple of shovels from us, then made a comfortable platform on which we could both stand with our feet on the wagon floor. As we were now on a full night shift of eight hours, commencing at 6.00 pm in the evening. We usually managed to toss out a further shovel or two before our shift ended. This allowed us to smoke, discuss all the topics, films, musical shows, families, the war, etc. The guards knowing, we were safely inside the wagons, were out of sight most of the time, trying to keep warm in their very thin grey coats, whereas we were protected by the sides of the goods wagon. Towards the end of our shift, we would leave the wagon of say 20 tons hardly disturbed for the next shift to take over. The Germans did not appreciate the interminable delay in the turn round of their wagons but that was their problem.

One night, we cleared our space as usual, lit up our cigarettes, and I opened the evening with a pleasant discussion on the stars and planets, with my engaging companion. All at once I heard the usual yelling and screaming, and saw on a high pile of beet where the wagons unloaded, and very near us, a horrible little German Unteroffizier with a fair copy of his master's moustache adorning his upper lip. He was accompanied by a guard. The German NCO grabbed the guard's rifle and fixed bayonet and charged down the slope of sugar beet, managing to keep his balance, into our wagon. Thrusting the bayonet into my stomach so that I felt the point, he screamed.

"Arbeit Oder Nicht".

The Germans always screamed. I hesitated, considering carefully my predicament.

"Arbeit Oder Nicht". Came another hysterical outburst.

Now the Unteroffizier was only half my size and probably much older than I was, yet he obviously made up for this great disadvantage, by possessing a loaded rifle, with a very sharp bayonet, which was giving him complete confidence. I slowly started to shovel beet as did my friend also; after two or three shovels, the NCO left the wagon. Unfortunately, I stopped shoveling too soon. He immediately rushed back to us giving a repeat of his pantomime. We made quite sure he was really gone after that. Apparently, this performance had gone on in all the wagons that night, and later we learned the reason why.

British Commandos had landed on one of the Channel Islands and taken a few German soldiers as prisoners. They had tied their hands behind their backs in order to get them into their boat, but the vessel capsized and the prisoners drowned. The Germans made a big propaganda exercise of this, and ordered all POW's. to have their hands tied. Now their dilemma was that they could not very well secure the hands of those working prisoners, such as me, but they could tie up all those not working in Lamsdorf. So, they procured chains, when that ran out, rope, and then string, probably from our Red Cross parcels and proceeded to tie up our comrade's hands. Of course, the lads freed themselves, as quickly as possible and rejoined the queue, thus the interminable process went on all day, and day after day until even the Germans realised the stupidity of such punitive treatment. We at the sugar beet plant, as all other working parties, were receiving the back-lash of this affair.

Again, I was offered a job, this time inside the warmth of the factory. The lad who recommended me and took me together with two other POW workers, did not refer to my previous employment, when handing us over to the civilian in charge. It was such a big place with so many POW's that nobody connected me with any other incident. I surveyed my two companions, one was Hughes that I already knew, he was a very cheerful person, with a happy smiling expression, and laughed a good deal, a tonic to work with. The other fellow was fairly tall, older than both of us, he wore two stripes on his uniform which meant he could have had genuine rank of Corporal, or more possibly a self-promoted position of "Stalag Corporal".

We were taken up the stairs to the second floor observing on our way, that there were some pretty Polish girls employed in various places. We reached a large empty highly polished floor on which were miniature railway lines, and on them three small very clean, well-oiled skips about waist height. In the centre of the floor beside the railway track a large part of the floor had been removed, revealing below a huge storage magazine on the floor of which was a great heap of unrefined brown sugar. In the corner of the room by the swing doors, was a metal chute, with a shutter closed over the aperture. Above the chute was a large bell, with a handle, and a warning notice. Apparently, the job consisted of the three of us in turn, pushing our respective skips under the chute. We then pulled aside the shutter and down would cascade brown sugar filling the skip very quickly, probably in half a minute. This shutter also rejected brown knobs of sugar, which we of course could take away with us, or even eat them, but after one or two, they inclined to make one feel queasy. Each man would immediately push his full skip around the floor to the opening, tip the contents down into the magazine, and return on the single circular track, to the waiting machine.

The guard watched us go through these trial run motions, bored with the whole proceedings, but no doubt delighted to be inside the cosy warmth of the factory, with nothing to do but sit down and take it easy, as no one would disturb us as long as the flow of sugar was tumbling down into the floor below. It was easy work, but a never ending process, for as soon as one skip filled, the other was at once behind, and as soon as you tipped your contents, so you caught up the man in front, just closing the shutter and going, ready for you. As it was afternoon when we commenced this merry-go-round, it was soon time to return to our quarters, so accompanied by the guard we left the works, loaded with sugar lumps for ourselves and friends, to put into our mugs of tea.

The next day as usual after morning roll-call, checking and counting, we all proceeded to the factory where every group split up with their various guards, to go to our respective places. We marched up the stairs with our guard, keeping a sharp eye open for the Polish damsels, reached our floor and entered. Just before we began our first full day on the sugar run trail, the "Corporal" asked the guard what time we would get our morning break. This time-honoured custom we had usually managed to extract from the Germans and of course if they were lax or forgetful, we would prolong this as long as possible. The guard shook his head, and told us, no break. This was a severe disappointment to us, for any pause in the working day was an enjoyable period.

I did not like the thought of a continuous performance, but pushed the skip along trying to put up with this misfortune. The "Corporal" however was not giving up that easily and began several times to induce the guard to agree to a break. The guard however was adamant. I heard the Corporal muttering aloud that if we did not soon get a break, he would pull the warning bell above the shute. Of course, Hughes and I grinned at this joke, because we had been informed that if an emergency occurred, and the bell was pulled the factory process came to a standstill, in view of this calamity.

The Corporal was muttering that he would pull the bell and as I was half-way round the floor with Hughes behind me, my back was facing the shute, when I suddenly heard the deafening ringing of a very loud alarm bell. I turned around in horror to see the Corporal standing by the bell, leaning against the huge mound of rejected lumps of sugar, which was propped at the sides by wood, calmly informing the panic-stricken guard that it was now break time. There was a stunned silence I looked at Hughes who was actually laughing. The swing doors burst open to reveal a German officer and NCO, another guard and civilians in white coats. They all started to shout and scream together. The Corporal leaning casually against the wooden barrier, was trying to shout that he wanted a break. Hughes was grinning like a Cheshire cat. I was crouching low behind my little skip for I felt that at any moment the shooting would start. They all rushed at the Corporal who went down on a heap of sugar, with the guard and the NCO, wrestling in the sugar. I thought this really was the end, we would never get away with this. The officer was screaming for order and gradually things began to get calmer. The Corporal got up covered with sugar and no doubt bruises, as did the NCO and guard. The officer with his veins bursting in his neck, yelled in German so quickly I could not follow his intentions, but we were seized by the Germans, and propelled out of the door and booted down the stairs, into the factory yard. There were cheers and laughter from every working POW when they saw our ignominious exit. We rejoined the labour squads with our forks, and kept them amused relating the happenings of our morning. Needless to say, I was not recommended for any further suitable employment, by the Germans at the sugar beet factory, due no doubt to my unsatisfactory references.

At the end of the season in early December 1942, we were on the move again. I had to say goodbye once more to my old Karlsthal friends, and join the Bransdorf party, consisting of the Aussies, New Zealanders, Scots and English lads bound for a new destination. Accordingly, we packed our belongings and marched to the nearest railway station to board our cattle trucks. I reminisced on the journey, remembering incidents, some amusing, some sad, over my two years of captivity.

I recalled a winter day when after snow clearing high up a hillside, returning along the only road, to see in front of us a large flat cart laden with felled trees, all chained securely.

The two German Waggoner's muffled against the intense cold, were trying to induce the team of four horses, to pull the wagon, which was stuck in frozen snow. Seeing their predicament our guards ordered us to help them by heaving and pushing the laden cart. Both guards were manning the front wheels, helped by the Waggoner's. I had one finger resting lightly on the load. The Germans were shouting, heaving and straining, their eyes bulging with effort, but I am sure none of us were pushing at all. At last with a desperate cry, the wagon rolled free and the exhausted Germans panted for breath. I personally was as fresh as a daisy, as most of the lads were too.

Another occasion called for us to be transported by a tractor as far as possible up a high mountain, named halt vater". At the top of this mountain was a radio tower which was short of fuel. It was intended that from a large heap of coke deposited there for just this sort of emergency, we would fill sacks provided, with seven shovels of coke, and carry them up to the tower. At first the sack seemed extraordinarily light, but as one climbed up to the top of the mountain, breathing became difficult, and the load seemed to get heavy. Inside the tower a German civilian shoveled the coke, as we tipped the sack, and then we slid down the steep slope in the snow towards the stockpile. There were one or two thick bushes growing through the deep snow and these were at the half-way mark and became very handy, to tip half our load of coke under, and bury, then stagger to the top with the remainder. In this way, the job was easily completed and with satisfaction we returned to board the tractor.

One of my friends, Harry Alderson[1], was chatting to a lad from another party of POW's that had joined us on this operation. He had been captured in Crete and his experiences like ours on becoming a POW were sad, so we understood what he had endured. Harry who did not smoke, used to exchange his cigarettes for chocolate, from the Red Cross parcel. He had a ¼lb bar with him, and suggested to me that he would like to give this to our comrade.

This was such a noble gesture, under those conditions, that when I saw him give the lad the chocolate, and the expression of gratitude from that hungry chap, I had to turn away, so that they could not see my emotion. Only those who have known hardships, would appreciate my feelings. I remembered other small details, and funny occurrences and passed the journey thinking about these.

[1] *Harry Alderson survived the war and had a career as a research chemist in the textile industry. He passed away in 2005 at the age of 86.*

The railway siding - In between sick parades

At last we reached our destination and alighted from our cramped cattle-trucks. I cannot remember the name of this working party, but I know we marched through a village and a mile or so from there; we reached our new camp. It consisted of one long wooden hut, surrounded of course by the usual barbed wire. It was situated on flat ground just off the only road, and bordered by a large grassy field. There was a smaller hut for the guards, another for our kitchen, to cook our soup. There were the usual wooden toilets and washing troughs, fortunately under cover. Inside our barrack were two-tiered bunks and an opening in the wall leading to the next room, and the next. I think each of the three rooms held about 22 men apiece. There was a smaller room for the Scots Sgt in charge, a medical orderly, two cooks, and two assistants to the Sgt. All these were classed as camp staff and worked inside the little camp.

Our work was about half an hour's march away to where, right in the open, there was a railway track with an up and down line, with a bridge over the track. On each side of the lines was a vast expanse of open country, finishing with the inevitable pine tree forests. It was the intention of the Germans to construct sidings at a point just before the bridge and for about 2-400 yards where there was a high bank on the right hand side. This would be dug completely away, levelled off and track laid, one up and one down to shunt wagons. It would only be a small siding and the job was controlled by a civilian foreman experienced in this type of work.

The idea was first to remove enough earth to give space to lay miniature railway lines, then to use nine large skips on these lines to transport the rest of the bank, as it was dug, to the dumping zone about 500 or 600 yards down the track. None of this would seem apparent to me when we first started work, but on looking back I can see the idea now. As was my usual custom, I gave my name to the medical orderly on his evening round, reporting sick for the next day. In the morning everyone would parade, the workers separate, from the small number of men sick.

The German Unteroffizier was a horrible little man, who would ferociously glare at the sick, whilst the count of all personnel was being agreed. As soon as the workers had departed and the small camp staff, gone about their duties, the German Unteroffizier would rush at the nearest man on sick parade, grab his hand, left or right, pretend to take his pulse and shout at him. "Was ist los" (What is going on?). Before the chap could reply he would boot him to one side, where a guard would be waiting to take him and the others to work. As the little fiend worked his way towards me, I stood rigidly upright. As he reached me, his eyeballs protruding, I would look down at him, click my heels, and shout. "Ich bin krank[1], Herr Unteroffizier"

[1] *I am sick*

He used to continue glaring at me for a few seconds, then he would push me aside as genuinely sick. Then I, together with the other fortunate's, not more than three or four of us, would be taken by another guard down to the village to see the Czech doctor. If one was lucky, a day off could be obtained, sometimes two whole days.

I suspect the doctor knew very well we were all shamming, but did his best for us, in view of the Germans. On returning from the doctor, back to camp, we were put to work, usually on the Unteroffizier's patch of ground, he fondly imagined was a garden.

Of course, I could not go sick too often just as frequently as possible, virtually every week or so. Other days I went to work. A space had already been cleared for the bogie tracks, which were laid, and our nine wagons required filling.

At this time in 1943, the guards were harvesting the first seeds of disillusionment, coupled with the few cigarettes, we doled out to them, all helped to make life easier, although they would hassle us, not too loudly but for the benefit of the civilian foreman. My skip was at the end of the line and assisting me to fill this, were two wonderfully lazy New Zealanders, a credit to their homeland. The front skip was manned by three Aussies who usually filled up quite fast, chatting cheerfully as they did so.

My method was slightly different. I would remark to my companions.

"Did you put in a shovelful"

"Yep, sure did" came the reply.

"Well I didn't see it"

"Neither did I, Lofty" would remark the other New Zealander.

I would wait to see if they moved, which after some time they did reluctantly putting a half-shovel into the skip. In that case I would follow suit. While this was laboriously progressing all the other skips would be full, the lads, chatting and smiling awaiting our skip, so that the line could move off. This compelled the guard and the foreman to concentrate on us. We would do our best to delay filling the skip, carefully calculating how far we could go, then at last we were all ready to move.

Each skip was pushed by the three man crew up the long gradient, and as soon as the first skip reached the top, one man would ride on the front iron surround and two at the back. The skip would gather momentum with the weight of the crew keeping it nicely balanced. On most occasions, the wagon would negotiate the bend at the bottom leading to the dumping site. The second skip would set off, following the same procedure, then would come our turn. This was really good fun for the skip would travel quite fast but somehow, we often came off at the bend. We knew instinctively that it was going and we used to leap for our lives, for the heavy skip if it had hit you would have done quite some damage. We would right the skip, helped by all the others, refill the spillage, and proceed. This slowed things down nicely of course, the others used to hurtle off at the bend, and the civilian would wring his hands in anguish, appealing to the guard, who would also help to right the skip. There was nothing anyone could do because it seemed so natural to us at any rate, and made our day so much more interesting.

Once as I leapt clear on the bend as the skip hurtled off, I felt a slight glancing blow on my knee, so as I rolled clear I starting yelling and moaning holding my knee. The lads all rushed up anxiously, as did the guards, but I whispered to them that I was only spoofing, and seeking to be taken back as sick. At that they broke down laughing so much, I had to abandon my plan, owing to the guard's bewilderment, so I limped away pretending it was not serious, and that I would carry on. I became fed-up with my two companions, who were disgustingly lazy, and not helping at all with the Fatherland's problem of improving railway communications. I decided to go sick that night and secretly told the medical orderly, so that the other two would not get wind of it. On parade the next morning, I heard hoots of laughter as the rest of the workers saw not only me, but the other two on my skip, had gone sick by sheer coincidence. Each of us trying to escape from the others. There were no other sick that morning and we all managed to survive the harassment of the German medical expert. Off we trooped to the doctor to try our luck. We were all examined and all given work. The guard marched us straight down to the work-site and as we approached, the skips were nearly all filled, except our last, solitary, empty wagon. Everyone was laughing, even the guards joined in, as we reluctantly took our places, for another day.

It was a good working party and I enjoyed again the friendship of everyone, although at this time I was once more on my own, preparing my meals, not having a partner, since Bill and I were separated. I was reasonably satisfied, Red Cross parcels were regular, mail was being received and dispatched. I now had at least two pairs of shoes, more would follow. I also had more clothes, a new battledress uniform, and I must pay tribute here to those wonderful anonymous people back home, who supplied the Red Cross with books specially purchased to send to us. This made all the difference to me, for I have always read widely, and now was enjoying such authors as Walpole, Trollope, Deeping and many others. I had just received "Gone with the Wind" which I intended to read as soon as possible.

The war news was much more hopeful, the Germans were badly in need of men, the guards were being replaced by older men, and best of all, our detestable little Unteroffizier had departed for the Eastern Front. How grateful I was to the Russians who had a remarkable propensity for disposing of objectionable or unreasonable Unteroffiziers, in a most satisfactory manner. The new German NCO arrived, and we learned that he had been badly wounded on the Russian Front. One of his arms hung limply by his side and one of his legs were obviously affected. He was a younger man, and we were informed a quieter type, which proved to be true.

As soon as this information was assimilated, and the Scots Sgt and medical orderly made their usual rounds to take names of those wishing to report sick, I immediately volunteered. The other lads in my room at once, rightly protested that I was always sick, and should give them a chance. Immediately I asked for my name to be deleted. To my surprise and admiration, our Scots N.C.O. who always encouraged us to go sick, which was an unusual attitude for those in charge of working parties, spoke up.

"Look here lads, this is unfair. Lofty has always gone sick, during the hard man's reign and it is only right that he continues now things might be easier".

"Lofty, I want you to put your name down again."

I thought that was extremely kind of him and the lads, to give them their due, instantly accepted this suggestion.

In the morning on sick parade, and there were quite a few budding hopefuls, I noticed a new guard who wore glasses, carefully studying the sick record book, which the methodical Germans maintained. I at first assumed he was more intelligent than the normal guard type, and I hope I was doing him a grave injustice. He approached our sick group and asked if "Herr Shorrock" was here. He was, and I stepped forward. He glared at me and jabbed his finger at my name, which I state in all due modesty appeared regularly on every page. He muttered my name over and over with amazement as he whisked through the book. He wagged his finger, rather nearer to my face than I desired, and remarked that he would see the doctor that morning about this state of affairs.

As we marched off towards the village and our ultimate fate, I whispered to the boys that I would obviously be sent to work. On reaching the doctor, I had not bothered to rehearse my act, so when I entered the surgery, I merely complained of stomach ache, the usual favourite. The doctor gave me a cursory examination and I was dismissed. The guard immediately went in and I soon heard the raised voices, which I judged was my case being discussed. The guard emerged, with a crestfallen face and approached me, saying the words that linger forever in my memory. "Du hast wiede zwei tage im barracke". You have again two days off!

I was delighted, the Czech doctor must have resented the guard telling him his job, which would be only natural anywhere. That is how I was able to read and complete "Gone with the Wind", a fascinating story of the old American South and the Civil War, that I simply was unable to leave.

The summer of 1943 was a good one and the first and only year I really achieved a tan to the waist as did almost everyone. Every day out working on our siding, trains would rattle past every now and again, slowing on the gradient. There were many coal trains, at the rear of which, in the guard's truck or compartment, stood attractive Czech girl guards, in a very smart uniform. You had to hand it to the Germans everyone connected with them had a uniform. Even the village postman looked an important personage dressed in his superb outfit.

We would wave to the girls who were always so charming to us. We would run alongside the train exchanging vows of love and impossible assignations, which everyone enjoyed hearing. The wounded trains came along frequently and they were usually full of Italian wounded, although I am sure there must have been Germans travelling on them as well. As the train appeared, we would get ready, drop our shovels, and run alongside the train hurling insults at the Italians.

"Which way were you running when you got hit".

"Was it in the backside".

"How could they have missed you".

"The Duce won't like this".

There were many more words too bad to mention here. At the rear of each train would be the German girl nurses, very smart and attractive who would wave deliberately, affectedly, and intentionally at the guards. We would pretend they were waving at us and would call out in German, those who could manage the remarks.

"Can't see you tonight, how about tomorrow".

"I'll write to you sometime".

"I am not married yet".

We would say anything else we could manage which used to infuriate them. The guards never bothered us much, only making a show, for they hated the Italians as much as we did. They knew that it was strictly forbidden for any POW to associate with Frauleins, even if they ever got an opportunity. It was the death penalty if you did. Who wanted to anyway, with all these charming Czech and Polish women, we sometimes saw. There were two express trains on the same route going to wherever that was, one at 4.40 pm the other at 5.40 pm I was standing on the railway bridge with two New Zealanders, doing something or other, but really spinning time away. I was awaiting the 5.40 pm which was almost due. About 50 yards away, standing with their backs to us and the oncoming train, was a German officer, possibly connected with railway transport, our Unteroffizier and the civilian foreman. As the train hurtled round the bend, behind us and came on, I suddenly gasped out to my friends.

"Look, they are busy arguing, they haven't noticed the train. I'd better warn them".

I involuntarily opened my mouth to do this, when like lightening, one New Zealander placed his hand firmly over my mouth, grabbing me-securely assisted by his friend.

"Shut your mouth, you bloody fool", one hissed.

I stared in muted horror as the train was almost on them, just in time they realised their peril and leapt clear, falling over in the process, with shock. Of course, all the lads were grinning, the guards never shouted out, maybe their attention was elsewhere. The Germans were livid, they knew no one had warned them and they were really cursing. I said to the others. "Would you really have let it happen".

"Of course," they replied. "There's a war on, you know". I have no doubt they would have done.

One night fast asleep in my top bunk, I heard a loud shot seemingly close to my ear. In the morning I found, for someone pointed out, a bullet was imbedded in the solid post, near where my head was resting inside. If it had entered the flimsy panel of the wall, this story might never have been written. I considered this another miracle. There would be others. I think possibly the guard on duty was either dreaming or chasing shadows, perhaps the Germans never heard it in their quarters for no action was seen to be taken although this was considered a serious offence in any army.

A surprise occurred one morning, for Charlie Crisp, of the Karlsthal party was brought to our camp, all alone. I was delighted to see him and eager to hear his story. He told me that recently a few of them had managed to get under the wire at night into the village at Karlsthal, where some Polish girls were billeted. Charlie, like the others, had taken them little gifts from their Red Cross parcels, such as soap, chocolate, cigarettes, etc. things these poor girls had been denied for so long. Charlie had fallen in love with one girl, and he described her to me in glowing terms. Unfortunately, quite by chance, he had been selected with some other POW to join a new party, and had thus been separated from his girl. Consequently, he had escaped, hoping that after his quick recapture, he would serve his sentence in Lamsdorf cells and then try to rejoin Karlsthal. His plan had gone wrong, for he was posted instead to us.

Escaping of course was the duty of any POW and full credit to the many thousands who did so. Now the chances of getting back for other ranks was extremely remote, although the RAF had many successes, and even the army from Colditz, and other camps. I had never attempted escape, although I once planned details with another lad, but our scheme was never allowed to be put into practice. I considered that my German was too poor, my height a drawback, for once seen by the Hitler Youth, or any armed service personnel, I was sure to be questioned. I also had no opportunity to get German money, or civilian clothes, but these excuses are not sufficient to disguise my selfish reason to sit it out, enjoying my parcels from home, letters, and Red Cross supplies. Many POW's escaped, but did this to get away from a bad working party, then on serving time in Lamsdorf, could apply for a different work Commando. The trouble was that at Lamsdorf there had been so many POW's registered that the camp could not accommodate probably more than say 10,000. The few punishment cells were always fully occupied by our splendid chaps, for various offences including escaping, but there were always hundreds of POW's awaiting their turn to serve their time. It was easy to see that after such long delays and bureaucratic methods by the Germans, a POW would find himself sent to join any working party.

Charlie informed me that he was determined to escape as soon as possible, to try and rejoin his girl by the described method. I tried to dissuade him by argument, pointing out that the Germans had now issued notices to every camp, stating that escaping was no longer a sport, and all POW's should now give up this exercise. This was mainly because of the marvelous tunnel escape, when 50 of those RAF escapers were recaptured, and murdered by the Gestapo. A mass escape as that had been, had put all the German military and civil home units on a vigorous alert which had caused great disorganisation. Charlie appreciated my concern, but was adamant about going. He had put the Scots Sgt in the picture and had elected to go out under the floorboards in my room, and out through the wire. Charlie was in my room as I knew him so well and when the chosen day for his departure had arrived we gathered in the dark after lights out, to ensure he got out safely. Before going Charlie had handed to me, his friend, his Red Cross tins of food, which he did not want to take, as he did not intend to remain at large long. In his case the idea was to put a few miles, as many as possible, as quickly as could be managed, so that in the event of a swift recapture, you were not brought back to the working party from which you had escaped. This was because the sentry on duty, when you vanished at night, was severely punished by three months in the cells, so naturally if you were taken back to that camp, you would almost certainly be beaten up.

I said goodbye to Charlie, very sadly indeed and after the floorboards had been removed, he vanished in the dark. We all waited breathlessly praying that we would not hear the shouts or shots from the sentries, patrolling outside the wire. The minutes ticked by, then a quarter of an hour, then half. A great sigh of relief came from those who had witnessed his departure, and we all crept silently into our bunks. Unfortunately, the Scots Sgt. came to me two days later with the bad news that Charlie had been apprehended and worse, was being brought back to our camp. He had managed about 17 miles, not bad at all. The Scots Sgt. told me that he was seeing the Unteroffizier immediately to ask him to treat Charlie correctly and not let him be beaten by the guards. The German kept his word, and Charlie was treated decently by his captors. I managed to return, via the Sgt, the tins of food he had given me and flatly refused to take them now under any condition. Charlie was taken away. I never saw him again. A fine, clean, upright, British lad, cheerful, a true friend and loyal companion. Later in the war I made many enquiries and heard that he again later escaped from a punishment camp, and had been shot. I could never confirm this, and I do hope he did survive, for such an end to a brave lad the same age as myself, would have been terribly sad.

Lamsdorf revisited - and out to Auschwitz

Working on the railway siding occupied my thoughts during those lovely warm summer days and was made bearable by the comradeship of all members of our working party. Out of the blue one day came an unexpected event. We were all laughing and chatting as we laboured on the siding, when we saw our Unteroffizier approaching with a civilian in a white coat. We were all ordered to stop work and stand in single file, while the civilian who was obviously a German doctor examined each of us. He would stand in front of each man, if necessary questioning the German N.C.O. He felt their arms, tapped their chests, examined their backs. He would push one or two lads to one side and continue down the line. I was almost last. I was feeling quite well and fit. I was very sun tanned, and not skinny as I was in 1940. The doctor stood in front of me, looked me over, he was a small man. He turned to the N.C.O. and said.

"Gut gebaut". Good Build.

He walked behind me, then examined my back wound for a few moments. He then gently pushed me to one side. The next day with the exception of five men including myself, all the rest of the working party were marched away to the German coal mines. We five were to return immediately to Lamsdorf, as unfit. Another miracle.

We packed our belongings and marched to the station, travelling by coach, with our guard on route to Lamsdorf. This was my second return to Stalag VIIIB.

On reaching Lamsdorf I was greatly surprised by the enormous difference since my last visit. Morale was high, men looked smarter. There were many Canadian soldiers captured in 1942, at Dieppe, and a whole compound of RAF shot down bomber crews, a few fighter pilots, a few officers destined to be sent to Stalag Luft camps. The Red Cross had supplied books to form a library, there was a tip-top dance band and other musicians. Rough games of cricket and football, baseball for the Canadians, Church services conducted by captured padres who elected to stay, and medical officers.

One of the first interesting sights, immediately after our daily roll-call was over, consisted of crowding as near as possible to the barbed wire to observe the daily roll-call of the RAF. They would stream out into their compound, and instead of getting into the correct three rank files, would form fours or fives, with the guards shouting. A German Officer waiting, trying to control his temper, together with German Feldtwebels and NCO's. When the RAF had formed three ranks, providing there was not a guard too near to observe the rear rank, a small man in the first file rear rank would wait until the guards had counted drei, sechs, neun, three, six, nine, he would then run along the rear of the file to the last position of two men and make another third. This confused the count, which was always incorrect anyway, so as the first tally was taken, supposing there were 250 men to make it easy. The first guard would rush up to the Officer, click to attention and bawl out 248 men. The next would rush up and shout "254 men". When the third person probably a German NCO rushed up with another figure, the German Officer, used to explode and start

160

screaming. As we were all grinning and jeering, matters got very tricky, the guards would wave their rifles at the RAF contingent, who were calling out insults, the pandemonium was a treat to watch, as long as it ended without violence. Usually one or two RAF were marched away to the cells, which had a terrific waiting list anyway, on account of their insolence. This was a happy start to each day.

I had not been back at Lamsdorf long when a friendly face appeared from the Karlsthal party. His name was Holt. Now Holt was a Londoner, very young, very smart, good looking, very sharp.

He always polished his boots, wore his gaiters, his uniform spick and span and would have delighted any R.S.M. Holt had one passion, namely boxing. He had shown a great interest in the noble art as soon as boxing gloves were available. He trained and practiced, was a quick learner and made wonderful progress. He was medium height, very fit, and he would take on anyone at the drop of a hat. In fact, you had to choose your words carefully when speaking to him, for he would take you up in an instant if he thought you were saying anything detrimental towards him. I was sitting at a table, discussing old times, he really was a nice chap when you knew him. A dour Scots lad came along and either trod on Holt's boot, or accidentally kicked him. Holt was up in a flash, words were exchanged, and Holt hit the other lad. A fight immediately ensued and I had a ringside seat.

At first, I thought to myself, this Scots lad who was broader and slightly taller than Holt, was in for a big surprise. Holt was weaving, parrying, ducking, slipping punches but then I noticed one little set-back, he was not winning. The Scots lad was as steady as a rock, he could take it and he could return it. After a long, long time for these bare fisted fights, the Sgt. Major in charge ordered a halt and the two antagonists shook hands in the usual sporting manner. When Holt regained his seat at the table, I complimented him on his excellent performance, but asked him what he thought of the other chap. He looked at me ruefully, before replying.

"I never thought he was that good. In fact, I was afraid he would get the better of me".

He looked very dejected. I think Holt had discovered the truth of that saying. There is always someone better.

I cheered him up by referring to an incident in the winter of 1940, when in the bitter cold, the Sgt. Major in charge of my barrack, would order everyone outside in the cold for an hour or two, ostensibly to clean up the barracks. We had no option but to obey, but I was fed up then and very, very hungry, so I tried to hide on my bottom bunk. The Sgt. Major saw me, ordered me to get up, then seized my collar at the back screwing it up tight. He grabbed the seat of my trousers, screwing them up also, and literally ran me down the barrack, my feet hardly touching the ground. As the windows whizzed by and I reached the open door at the end, I sailed through the air and landed on a big heap of snow. For some reason I started to laugh as I recalled the old silent movies, and thought was a splendid scene that would have made, but I would not want to do a re-take. A lad passed by who saw this incident, commiserated with me, and shouted at the departing Sgt. Major.

"Every dog has his day".

These words soon came true for the Sgt. Major tried the same trick on another lad subsequently, and this lad got down from his bunk and gave him a good hiding. He had picked on the wrong man. Holt laughed at this and I am glad he saw the point, as I hoped he would.

The R.A.F. were not allowed to go out to work as other ranks were compelled to do so. Some genius invented the wonderful idea of changing identities. This is how it was arranged. An army soldier would approach an RAF type, or vice-versa and agree to swap. They each would exchange the necessary information as to where they were captured, or shot down, learn these details thoroughly, and then change uniforms, by that of course I mean, there were plenty of uniforms now available, and personnel skilled in tailoring to adapt them. So the soldier became an RAF airman and took over the bed and position he occupied. The real RAF type would don army battledress, become a private soldier and go into the army other ranks compound. He would then apply to join the first available working party, go out on that, bide his time, until an escape attempt occurred. It was rightly considered that the RAF had the better chances of success due to their intelligence, education, etc, and they all performed marvelously. If the RAF type did reach home, which happened in some rare cases, he would send parcels of cigarettes to his swop in Lamsdorf.

The snags were, that if by some misfortune the RAF man posing as a soldier escaped, was recaptured, and not returned to Lamsdorf, but to a different camp, or worse still if he was sent direct to the German coal mines, his swop would have to retain his false identity for the duration of the war.

Another problem was that if the army soldier kept in the RAF compound posing as a flyer, grew tired, or bored, waiting for his swop to escape and return to change into their correct identities. He would then, in some cases, approach another unsuspecting army POW and suggest changing identities with him, subsequently, if agreed, disappearing on a working party. This meant that when the original changeover escaped, was recaptured, and returned to Lamsdorf, he would seek out his substitute in vain. He would then be compelled to wander about asking himself, "Who am I".

It was a wonderful idea to change, because it gave the POW soldier a chance to rest for a long period in Lamsdorf, and the RAF, golden opportunities for "Veglaufen", escape.

I once came across a group of soldiers listening in admiration to a description of a dogfight in the air, being given by a New Zealand Air Force Officer. It was an enthralling tale, which I stopped to enjoy also. As the flyer got on to the Messerschmitt and fired off his guns at the enemy, I detected one slight flaw in the narrator's tale. I recognised the airman, as a New Zealand solider named Wagstaff. At that moment, he caught my eye, instinctively knowing I had recognised him, but with superb composure carried on finishing his exciting story. When the little group had dispersed, I approached Wagstaff, who then told me in confidence of the swop over system. He had never set foot in an airplane.

I decided to get in on this procedure, the obvious answer to avoid working any more for the Germans. Lamsdorf to me now was a far better place to be, why I even saw a film, with Judy Garland and Mickey Rooney in the Andy Hardy Series, where Judy sang "Happy Birthday". I found a Canadian Flying Officer who was delighted and eager to swop with me, but before this could be finalised, the Germans spiked my guns, by having the audacity to send me towards the end of 1943, out to another working party. This time, Auschwitz.

Before I relate the details of this episode, I must mention that I saw the fair-haired anti-tank gunner, who I had first met at Hesdin. He now had a camp job at Lamsdorf, and I saw him playing in a football match, so knew he had recovered from his wound successfully. We exchanged the usual greetings when we met. I also ran into Bill Telford, whom I was extremely pleased to see, but very sorry to learn that he had been returned to Lamsdorf due to an accident, in which he had lost part of a finger on one hand. The other person I also encountered was Les Parry of Karlsthal, who was at Lamsdorf, on private business connected with his family. It was such a pleasure to meet old friends, and of course many I knew vaguely by sight from 1940 days at Lamsdorf.

Repatriation of disabled and very ill POW's had been on and off and subject to acute and bitter disappointment. I appeared before the Board consisting of Senior British Medical Officers, Swiss Red Cross Officers and German Representatives. I knew I had not the faintest chance of succeeding and my examination took about 30 seconds, whereupon I was curtly dismissed. Still it was worth a try.

I next saw Dusty Miller who was a Southern Irish, British soldier, older than I and unwell with a stomach complaint with which he had suffered on our Karlsthal party. He was delighted to see me and gave out the wonderful news that he had been successful with the Repatriation Board and would shortly be returning home. As I congratulated him, yet sorry for the circumstances under which he was returning, he asked me to give him my home address so that he could write to my mother and tell her how well I was. I did this at once, thanking him but secretly realising that in the heady atmosphere of being reunited with his loved ones, it would be perfectly understandable, for him to forget to write, or perhaps mislay the piece of paper I had given him. To my great astonishment and pleasure when I eventually returned, I discovered he had written a wonderful letter to my mother, not only saying I was well, but praising me for my cheerfulness and friendliness to all and assuring her I would soon return. My mother told me how happy she had been to receive such a letter and I say, God Bless dear old Dusty Miller, who kept his word, when I would never have complained, had he not.

The Germans at Lamsdorf were thoroughly dismayed. Here they had thousands of POW's in the camp and outside on Working Parties scattered in a rough radius of 50-100 miles. All their methodical records it seemed were unable to assist them when it came to finding the culprits they were seeking. The punishment cells were full. The barracks containing 200-300 men awaiting their turn for serving punishment was a mystery, for when they entered and called out the number of the unfortunate victim, no one responded, and no one could find him. They could not account for many prisoners and they were looking for at least 50-60 criminals? A criminal of course was a POW who has insulted the Third Reich, or its leader, committed acts of vandalism, theft of property, sabotage, and many other acts for which they demanded retribution.

One very cold morning in October 1943, when the snow was quite a few inches deep, I awoke early to the sound of many marching feet, coming it seemed, into the camp. There were immediate cries of "apell apell", roll-call, as men tumbled out of their bunks. Usually roll-call took only five to ten minutes and we could return inside again. This morning I was very suspicious and put on a heavy pullover, under my army greatcoat, then my socks and shoes. Many of the lads were dressed only in pyjamas, or shirt and trousers, some without their greatcoats. As we tumbled out we saw at once lines of German air force guards, tables were being brought into every compound; sentries were being posted at each barrack room door and entrance. There were Germans everywhere, clerical workers, fatigue workers in their black overalls, German Officers, Feltwebels and Underoffiziers. This was no ordinary roll-call. We were neatly trapped. Some lads attempted to go back and obtain food, some were successful, most were not.

The tables were set up and every man had to approach singly. First his Stalag number, worn on a metal disc round his neck, was checked against his record. Next, he was fingerprinted. His photograph on first registration was compared with the original person. Questions were put to him. Finally, he was allowed to go, but not back into the barracks, no one was to go in there.

It took all day in the freezing cold, nothing to eat or drink. Only the wooden open-ended toilets offered us any shelter. My turn came towards 3 or 4 o'clock in the afternoon as it was getting dark, when finally, we all returned to our barracks, completely frozen. The Germans found about half of the men they were looking for, but how anyone evaded that net is a mystery to me, but they certainly deserved the highest praise. Having put this now behind me, I was looking forward to spending the rest of my days in captivity, quietly reading, taking exercise, eating as much as I could obtain; listening to the excellent band or hearing plays, that were acted superbly I thought. As I have mentioned the Germans, now desperate for my extraordinary talents, called out my Stalag no. 17063, together with many others. We were off to Auschwitz.

To Reigersfeldt - Another synthetic petrol plant

There was quite a large party destined for Auschwitz, probably near the 300 mark, as we marched the familiar route, about November 1943, towards Lamsdorf Station, to board our salubrious cattle-trucks. After a journey of four or five hours, enduring the inevitable shunting, we arrived at the station, detrained and marched to our new camp. It was a very large camp seemingly set in an uncultivated muddy field, with the ever present barbed wire enclosure patrolled by guards. There were several wooden bungalows, each divided inside by a long corridor, with rooms on either side, containing the usual two-tiered bunks. The camp was reputed to be able to house about 1,000 prisoners. The majority of the men had been brought from Italy, after the collapse of Mussolini. They had endured bad treatment from the "Eyeties", not receiving regular supplies of Red Cross parcels or mail, as we had enjoyed.

A few miles away was the oil refinery, where we were to be employed, and also to meet and learn from the inmates of the infamous Auschwitz concentration camp, many of whom were forced to work in the plant as well. I, at this stage and virtually for the past two years had been on my own, not having found a suitable partner to share my food supplies with and of course frequent moves, had rendered this difficult. Our room held about 22 men, as did approximately all the others. One lad I became friendly with was named Maxie. He was a broad and powerful looking chap, with the stamp about him of a fighter.

When I got to know him better, he told me he had earned his 'living in the fairgrounds, before the war, taking on all challengers.' You had to be very tough and good for this sort of occupation.

I will refer again to Maxie. I soon made the acquaintance of two inseparable POW'S who were partners, but of totally different make-up. They were in another but not far from ours. Bert Smith came from Reading. Len Harvey came from Catford, quite near me. Bert was of medium height, about my age of 23, he was a quick-witted, intelligent person, with a very cheerful disposition.

Len was a big chap, who had been wounded in the foot, and sometimes often stumbled. He was very quiet, and devoted to Bert who usually made the decisions. I found them a fascinating pair, eager to do as little as possible, working as POW's and born ingenious skivers. I am proud to have been associated with them.

Before I became friendly, I went to work with all the other POW's to see what difficulties we had to contend with. Our first day at this huge refinery was a shock, for it was an enormous plant, built on concrete foundations, with gas holders, large workshops, uncompleted buildings, huge long steel gantries, chimneys smoking; railway sidings, sheds and huts. A far greater shock was our first encounter with the concentration camp victims, pathetically thin, dressed in their dirty, grey, striped pyjama-looking uniform with their appropriate coloured star sewn on the jacket. An American speaking inmate in perfect English greeted us, begging for cigarettes, to keep him as he said; from the gas chamber.

I was horrified as were my comrades to learn what was going on in the grim horror of Auschwitz. The American soon put us wise. He said if he could give the Kapo[1] in his block cigarettes each day, the Kapo would keep him off the death squad. So, he was supplied by our men. Some of these pitiful, obviously ill people were not fit enough to work and were terribly treated. I began to seriously wonder what might happen to us if the Germans decided to treat us in this sort of fashion. It was unthinkable.

I felt a feeling of gloom and despondency soon, working in this dreadful place, so I started my usual sick parade performance. It was during the days off sick that I began to make a plan to avoid work after observing the routine. The system was, that each morning the workers paraded, less the considerable number of men employed within the camp, and of course the sick. Let us assume there was really exactly a thousand men in the camp, and 750 went out to work. The Germans now had to agree the 250 left inside the camp, so all men sick or employed lined up in the corridor in three ranks for the count. While awaiting the German officers and NCOs who were checking other huts, I would stand anywhere in the rear rank with my back touching the door handle of a room, any room.

The Germans would enter with the Senior British Sgt. Major and his assistant to verify our numbers. There ought to be in our hut this day, say 35 men, but with me there was 36.

[1] *A kapo or prisoner functionary was a prisoner in a Nazi concentration camp who was assigned by the SS guards to supervise forced labour or carry out administrative tasks.*

As soon as the Sgt. Major read out to the Germans that he had in this but 25 men employed in the camp, and ten sick, I would unobtrusively open the door behind me, get swiftly inside and shut the door.

The Germans would count and find the number correct and walk out. The only danger lay in the guard not being near enough or cute enough to know what was happening. It worked like a charm. I do not know how many days I avoided work, but one day, I saw another lad watching me closely. The next day this same lad slipped in to the room I had chosen, with me. It had to happen. Other fellows discovered my secret and soon I found myself in a room with lots of lazy skivers. The end came when one of the guards decided to check the room to see now many sick were actually in bed. He found us all. Explanations were demanded but we were lucky we were all only marched down to the refinery.

It was then that I met Bert and Len and I told them about my antics and laughed. Suddenly, Bert came up with a wonderful idea. He pointed out that the camp was fairly new, and nobody really knew anybody else too well. He suggested that the three of us march out to work but when we entered the refinery, all the prisoners split up into various gangs of different numbers and marched away with their various guards to their working sites, many sites in view of each other. To belong to a particular gang, you were supposed to give your Stalag Number, to the appropriate civilian foreman, but Bert and Len had never done this. He reckoned that if we simply walked away as the gangs dispersed, each of us picking up a piece of odd metal pipe, not too heavy of course, each guard would imagine we were with some other group.

The whole factory was sealed off and patrolled by the SS outside, so the guards were not worried about anyone attempting to escape. It was brilliant. I enthusiastically agreed as did Len.

The first morning we attempted this ruse, it worked perfectly. We spent a pleasant day, choosing suitable hide-aways, in which to brew our morning and lunch time tea. Each day we sought means of improving our conditions, one of the first being, that we discarded carrying metal parts, instead we chose lighter pieces of wood. I had a classic example of Bert's presence of mind one day; when walking with him between two buildings, one of which was a factory. A guard unobserved some way behind us shouted out to us that he wanted us. As I involuntarily turned my head, Len seized me by the arm and quickly propelled me through the open shutters of a factory and out the other side. When we emerged safely, laughing with excitement, I turned to Bert and queried his action.

"Never look round Les, he wanted us for a job", answered Bert immediately.

My admiration for Bert was increasing steadily. We must have got away with our work dodging for nearly two months, when suddenly a tragedy occurred.

It was very cold and icy; probably February 1944, when as we were perambulating around the plant, passing various small groups of POW's working, a lad ran up to me saying

"I'm so glad you are safe, lofty. A prisoner has been shot dead, and I thought it could have been you".

We heard the story from many other comrades. What had happened was that a prisoner older than I was had been ordered to climb on to an icy steel gantry and he had refused. Without any warning, a young Nazi Feldwebel, had pulled out his pistol and killed him. We were completely shocked and devastated by this terrible news. The whole Auschwitz commando was seething with rage and indignation. Attempts at protests were made by the Senior Sgt. Major in charge.

Bert, Len and myself immediately on return that night, held a Council of War. The first matter to be decided was what should we do about our not working with any group. Bert stated that in his opinion we should join a group, an easy thing to do, for prisoners often interchanged to work besides their friends. I completely agreed with this policy, but I also said that Auschwitz now, with all that we had heard concerning the Jewish slave labour and their wicked treatment, coupled with the latest diabolical act of murder, had made me so depressed that I wanted to get away. Bert and Len were in complete agreement with me, and felt the same foreboding of disaster permeating that awful place. We decided no matter what happened, we would volunteer for any working party that the Germans demanded should leave Auschwitz. We fervently hoped it would not be to the coal mines.

So we went to work, and had no difficulty in joining one of the various groups in the factory. The German mentality could not really conceive that anyone would deliberately

174

avoid the tremendous honour of working for the Third
Reich. One evening we were lining up to return home to the
camp, in the cold wind and were anxious to be on our way.
We were held up by a tall, broad Egyptian looking prisoner,
who was in the British Army, but spoke with an accent. He
was chatting to the guards in a friendly manner, not
serving any purpose, for we had finished work and only
wanted to go. I was standing next to Maxie, my friend, the
fighter. Several lads called out to the big fellow to get into
line, but he ignored them. Maxie bellowed out. "Get back in
the ranks you Big bastard".

The big lad at once rushed over to where we stood, and
demanded to know who had addressed him. Maxie coolly
repeated the words. The fellow made a move towards
Maxie, which of course was annoying because of the
attention of the guards, who would never allow a fight to take
place. Maxie said to him.

"I'll deal with you when we get back".

As we commenced the long march home, I chatted away
cheerfully to Maxie naturally assuming that the incident
had now been forgotten. So evidently had the big chap,
for when we had entered the camp and been counted in,
we dispersed quickly for our quarters. Maxie ran after the
trouble-maker, grabbed his arm and told him he wanted to
see him further along the grass between the barracks. I
followed anxiously anticipating that sparks were about to fly.
Maxie faced the big chap.

"Put up your hands", he said.

There was no mistaking the grim purposeful stance Maxie adopted. The big chap complied. Instantly. wham! wham! The big chap was flat on his back in a state of complete shock, and bewilderment. I had never seen anything like that before. Maxie glared down at his opponent.

"Get up, I haven't started on you yet".

I took a grave risk, and intervened. I grabbed Maxie by the arm, and he began to push me away. I pleaded with him, pointing out the big fellow had already had enough. In fact, he did not seem capable of regaining his feet. Maxie at last yielded reluctantly to my persuasion and we returned towards our barracks. I took one last look back, but the big chap was very slow to rise.

I was getting more anxious to get away from Auschwitz. I felt something awful was going to happen and it did after I left. The Germans demanded a work force of about 300 men. We three; Bert, Len and I put down our names for this commando. We left the large camp at Auschwitz without any sadness at all, I, like the others, could not travel fast enough. We were taken in the familiar cattle-trucks destined for a job, which would be my last for the accursed Fatherland.

We could not have travelled a great distance from Auschwitz, perhaps 40 or 50 miles, but this time the name of the place will never leave me. It was Reigersfeldt. There was a huge complex of three IG Farben Industrie oil works, producing petrol and other chemicals for the German war machine. The outlook was much better. Our plant was built on sandy soil and the whole factory area was surrounded by pine trees. Far beyond them lay the other benzine plants, which of course we could not possibly see. This plant had similar buildings that we had seen at Auschwitz, but the powerhouse built of red brick, had two very tall slender chimneys at either end. Walking along the steel gantries, which stretched for a considerable distance, one had the feeling of being in the middle of nowhere. There was, however, very ominous signs. Construction of large above earth, solid concrete shelters, were well in progress, with a basement and two floors. There were two or three of these being built in various parts of the factory. It was said that they could withstand a direct hit by a 500lb bomb, but I had no wish to discover the veracity of that.

I found a new partner, a Welsh Guardsman named Harry Evans. He was a tall intelligent person about 27 years of age. We liked the same things, reading music, cinema, and we got along famously. Harry had a lovely sardonic chuckle, that I would hear, as lying on the underneath bunk, with Harry above, the lads would be discussing some subject, that we disagreed with.

"Hear that Les", he would call to me.

"Yes, Harry, unbelievable isn't it", I would reply.

I could rely on Harry to come out with firm commonsense remarks, that I am confident the other chaps listened to. So I was quite contented. Harry preferred to work on the particular job he volunteered for, but I spent my working days with Bert and Len, enjoying another period of the ruse we had employed at Auschwitz. I spent a lot of time in the evening with Bert and Len in their barracks, and I once asked Bert about his companionship with Len, who was such a complete opposite.

"Leslie; I promised Leonard, I would get him back safely one day to his dear old Mum", he said.

I was quite certain that if it was humanly possible, he would.

The bombing of Reigersfeldt, and us

'I escape' to Lamsdorf

Our barrack at Reigersfeldt was situated at the extreme end of the benzine plant. It had a small barbed wire enclosure and I think there were three or four huts. We were receiving regular supplies of Red Cross parcels and I had quite a lot of clothing at least two or three pairs of shoes, sent in my three monthly personal parcels from my family. The Red Cross packed these, removing and substituting any item that they thought the Germans might confiscate. The spring weather of 1944 was coming in, so we were looking forward eagerly to the approach of summer, and the long awaited invasion.

We somehow managed to keep fairly up to date with the news, knowing not only in Europe, but also in the Far East the war was slowly being won, at a terrible price in men and materials. We decided to obtain a fairly easy job that was required at the edge of the factory, so Bert, Len and myself joined this small labour force. All around the factory the Germans had placed, at various points, black metal barrels. These were maintained and operated by Luftwaffe personnel and gave out clouds of billowing white smoke, that covered the whole factory in an effective mist at ground level. This was a device against air attack by the allies. They also had dispersed in the woods, in clearings, many Flak Batteries.

So far, we had not seen any aircraft of a hostile nature, but now, on at least two occasions, Mosquito[1] reconnaissance

179

aircraft circled the whole area of the factory, as seen by the vapour trails made. Once they caught the Germans napping and despite their attempts to make smoke, the whole factory lay clear below our aircraft. We did not at that time pay any significance to these surveys, and the Germans never bothered to sound the air raid siren. The news of the Invasion of Europe on 6.6.1944, reached us almost immediately and at first progress of the allied forces seemed to our impatient anticipation, very slow.

In Italy the allies had long ago captured Foggia air base and were now positioned to make their long-range penetration of the German chemical petrol industries that had so far escaped their attention.

On a number of occasions, whilst at work, the air raid siren had been sounded, the smoke barrels discharged their fog, but no aircraft had approached the factory. One lovely summer morning at about 11 o'clock, Bert, Len and I were making our tea on a primitive twig fire. We brewed the tea in cocoa tins, and then poured it into our mugs. We were gaily chatting, sitting down waiting for the water to boil when the smoke barrels started to emit their white vapour, soon covering the factory area. Then the air raid siren sounded, but we took no notice of this as before. Suddenly, in the wood a Flak Battery opened up, and our look of surprise was immediately heightened by the sound in the distance of powerful synchronised engines. Bert was up in a flash, dragging Len, running towards the pine trees a hundred yards away.

[1] *The de Havilland DH.98 Mosquito is a British multi-role combat aircraft with a two-man crew.*

I quickly followed, the rest of the lads and the guards also. The noise of the aircraft became much louder and sounded extremely menacing. Just ahead of me was a slit trench that had previously been prepared by the Germans. It was covered by a thin layer of concrete and earth on top, but of course would only stop shrapnel splinters. At the entrance to the shelter stood a German Feldwebel, waving casually to anyone who cared to go into the trench. Bert ran past this haven with Len, turning his head to shout to me.

"In the woods, Les, in the woods".

Most of the lads were piling into the shelter and in a split second, I had to decide, either the woods with Bert and Len, or the shelter. I shot inside the trench and crouched down with the others. Immediately came the roaring sound of a four-engined aircraft screaming down. There was a blue flash and the pounding of bombs, my ears sang, and for some moments I felt disorientated.

We sat in the shelter listening to other distant vibrations, hoping the factory was completely destroyed, but praying we would emerge unscathed. At last the all-clear siren wailed, and we emerged to gaze across towards the factory, for the man made fog was clearing, but we were unable to see any damage. The powerhouse chimneys were still there which was a great disappointment to us. From the woods came staggering Bert and Len and as they did so, we noticed that quite near our shelter were the deep craters of a stack of bombs. I started to explain to Bert why I had not joined him in the woods, but he patted me on the shoulder and whispered to me that they had been unfortunate. Apparently, the American plane had dropped those bombs near the shelter as it was crashing, and Bert and Len were lying as flat as possible on the ground. Bert said he felt as if all the air was being pushed out of his body, for the plane crashed just in front of them. Bert immediately ran to the plane and found only one person, a 19 year old American lad who died within seconds of Bert reaching him. Bert removed his wristwatch, which he showed me secretly.

I asked him why he had done this and he replied.

"Les, as soon as the Germans get there, they will take anything like this, but I have a chance, after the war all being well, to try and return it to his family".

I marveled at Bert's presence of mind, for I am certain I would never have thought of doing that.

That night we were awoken several times by the sound of unexploded bombs intended to discourage workers from returning to the factory. When we resumed work in the morning we found that the plant had not been very badly damaged, due to the nature of the sandy soil on which it was built. It did not have the effect it would have at Auschwitz, where unfortunately, the factory was built on concrete, and the blast caused several deaths and casualties, among our POW's. How right we were to get away from that gloomy place, especially now, for as the air raids had begun, they were unable, at Auschwitz to get out because of the high wire fence all around the plant.

In the next few days, whenever the smoke was discharged and the air raid siren sounded, we headed for the woods. The guards were as eager as we to obtain cover, and being with us, the Germans could not possibly accuse us of attempting to escape, which they never did in this case. Our planes did not always appear, although the warning had been given, so we relaxed, not bothering to run more than fifty or sixty yards into the woods. It could not have been more than a week when the siren sounded, and we rushed into the wood. This time they came and caught us unaware, for they made their bombing run towards us discharging their deadly cargo, which came whistling down like an express train. We were lucky for as we emerged from the woods after this raid we could see the bomb craters in the sandy soil stretching in a line towards the factory, and to our camp. We immediately marched back to our small camp to find it had been bombed.

Slit trenches had already been dug sometime before and all personnel, such as sick and camp staff, had got into them, putting blankets, folded over their heads to minimise concussion, as advised by our medical officers. This undoubtedly helped to save lives, for no one was badly hurt, only severely shaken. Where my bed stood and the wooden hut we occupied, was now a 20 foot crater and matchwood. The bomb had fallen at the rear of the hut, just where my bunk and Harry's was situated. In the raid I lost everything, all my clothes, personal possessions, photographs and Red Cross food.

Some of the lads recovered things belonging to them, but all I found at the top of the crater was a torn snapshot, one of several sent to me. This was a calamity, and looking at the mess our small camp was in, it was obvious we would have to be moved out. We waited patiently as all the lads returned to camp to stare in amazement at the barrack, which had virtually ceased to exist. Although the others were devastated, and gaping holes torn through the remaining woodwork, we had fared the worst. In the late afternoon, we were ordered to get ready to move. We lined up, were counted, then those who had possessions carried them, and off we marched.

To my astonishment we were only marched about two hundred yards up the sloping road to another small civilian camp site, where the Germans were busy clearing the people out.

That night we slept on a concrete floor in the washroom and toilets. The next day we occupied the wooden barracks that also contained the usual two-tiered bunks. The main difference between this camp and ours was the proper lavatories that we enjoyed for the first and only time as POW's. We all discussed the implications of this raid. Everyone naturally expressed the fervent wish not to be eliminated by the U.S.A.A.F[2] at the same time hoping that we would see more destruction levied on the plant. It felt a little like sitting on the end of the branch one was sawing. We all decide to invoke that time-honoured maxim "Distance Beats Depth". In other words, whenever the air raid warning sounded, to run as far as possible during the time allowed before the bombing commenced.

A few days later, unfortunately, Bert, Len and I were sent to another part of the factory to collect some pieces of wood that could easily be carried.

[2] *The United States Army Air Forces was the military aviation service of the United States of America during and immediately after World War II, successor to the United States Army Air Corps and the direct predecessor of the United States Air Force*

On the point of making our way back to our work group the alarm went off. We now had the unenviable choice of using the large concrete shelters that the Germans had built above ground in the factory.

We quickly slipped inside where it was very dark and selected a corner away from the German civilian labour force. Bert whispered to us that if we kept quiet, the Germans would not know we were there, and so avoid the possibility of being ordered up to the top level, where we might discover the truth, as to whether these shelters were capable of surviving a direct hit.

The bombers came announcing their intentions by their deliveries, but our shelter was not hit. We were thankful to emerge after the raid and quickly made our way back. I paused near a railway line which was used to shunt materials into the factory and was chatting to Bert.

Up the line, a hundred yards or so, was a cattle-truck in which were French forced labour workers, unloading materials. They waved madly to us, and I waved back. They kept on waving, and then we both turned around to see an enormous U.X.B sticking about 8 feet out of the ground. For less than a split second my feet refused to act, but we were off like champion greyhounds streaking for home. There were many U.X.B's dropped in these raids, and unless you knew where they had fallen, there was always the danger of an explosion.

It was now nearing the end of July 1944, and I was passing a small building not far away from our work site, which was close to the woods. I heard over the German radio that heavy enemy bomber formations were approaching the Danube. I informed other work groups near at hand, and hastened back to my own party and gave them the news. We were halfway up the road, for it was better going than tripping over obstacles in the pine forests. We were dragging the guard along with us, trying to induce him to match our speed when the warning sounded. Within seconds, a lorry came speeding along the road away from the factory, so I put up my hand hopefully. It stopped. It was empty, being driven by a forced labour Italian worker. We all climbed aboard and the lorry sped away at an astonishing speed mile after mile, until I was seriously considering whether the greatest danger came from the anticipated raid, or the reckless progress of the vehicle. We finally stopped on a tiny road, miles from anywhere. There were small trees lining the road which provided excellent cover, if indeed, that had ever been required. We could hardly see the factory so far away it appeared, just the barest vague outline of the taller buildings.

The raid commenced with the faint drumming vibration of the earth. We strained our eyes to see from our grandstand view, the tiny silver silhouettes in the morning summer sun. It must have been half an hour we waited, and then the planes began coming out; heading towards us. The roar of their engines grew louder and more intimidating as they approached and I thought their formations were quite good in groups of fives and threes. I sincerely hoped that they had expended all their bombs, not reserving one or two just for us. In the nearby woods, a Flak Battery opened up with devastating effect and we all observed with horror, direct hits on a formation. The first plane exploded with a brilliance that seemed for an instant brighter than the sun. Nobody escaped by parachute. The second plane was hit immediately after, and then the third, with the same terrible effect and no visible escape by the crews. We were stunned by the appalling loss of three four-engined fortresses. Others may have been damaged but we could not tell.

After the planes had almost vanished we climbed aboard the lorry and were driven back to our boarding point. As we left the lorry, we looked at the factory and gave a muted cheer, for one of the red brick chimneys had been demolished. We hurried back to the camp, where there was jubilation from all our comrades as reports of fair damage began to arrive. Of course, some of the other lads in their various parties who although, running as far as possible into the woods, were naturally more nearly on the receiving end of the bomber's loads. I was getting a bit tired of this constant scrambling for safety, for we did this on many days when the air raid alarm sounded, but the planes did not appear. The only good thing we had was the knowledge that virtually little work was now being performed for our captors.

I told Bert and Len I would go sick in the camp for a few days, and enjoy the rest, catching up on my reading. This was now very easy, as nobody except the small camp staff, who had no choice anyway, wanted to be confined within the tiny barbed wire enclosure of the camp. There was a slit trench with forms to sit on so that our heads were just below the level of the earth sides. A thin layer of concrete covered the top, upon this was placed a layer of earth. Outside the wire the constant patrolling sentry had been provided with a solid concrete inverted cone, with an opening for him to get in. It looked safer in some ways than the trench we would occupy, but on the other hand we had company.

I saw two or three raids out in the camp shelter and took with me a guitar, quite a nice one, which the owner, like me, could not play but was happy for me to try and preserve for his benefit.

So in the raids, I strummed my three chords, C, D7 and G, while we all kicked up a row trying to sing songs. The guard in his concrete cone, could obviously hear us, but whether that offered him any consolation, I do not know, neither did I care.

We emerged from the slit trench one day after a raid, and as we searched the sky, we saw with some excitement, an American airman floating down to earth, mirrored in the beautiful blue cloudless sky. We saw that it looked as if he could land in our little compound, and we were willing him to do so. The Germans also had their eyes glued to this intrepid airman. Just as it seemed certain he would land among us, the breeze carried him gently about one hundred yards away from the wire. The German Unteroffizier, in charge of us immediately set his two guards running out to bring him in. As they quickly returned with their captive, they passed close to the wire of our camp. They were also dragging a civilian, probably a forced labour worker with them.

The American was a young, tall man, dressed in the typical flying suit and boots. He was carrying either a helmet or head cover of some sort, which he had obviously removed, as the left hand side of his face was bleeding profusely, from a deep gash by the top of his temple. As the guards escorted the flyer and the civilian into the guard room, where the Unteroffizier awaited them, we could clearly see through the wide open window, the guards hitting the civilian with their rifle butts, knocking him down. We were intensely alarmed, imagining that they would start next on our American ally. At once our Sgt. took our medical orderly, complete with his first aid box, to the Germans, asking permission to treat the airman's wound. The Unteroffizier allowed this and also agreed that the airman could receive a cup of coffee and biscuits from our Red Cross supplies, which was accordingly brought to him. Apparently, the civilian had tried to steal the parachute, which was the reason for his manhandling. Soon an ambulance appeared and the American was taken to hospital, so he was treated well and correctly. I often wondered what he thought on landing on enemy soil, to receive treatment from English speaking friends and Canadian coffee and biscuits. Harry and I had many discussions on the war situation, as we now understood the information received by us in August 1944. Everywhere, the Germans were on the retreat and the end of the war must be very near. I was now 24 years of age, well into my 5th year of captivity. I also talked to Bert and Len, about our present situation, for I had now decided to rejoin them, as I considered the cramped confines of our compound, left no opportunity to put as much distance between ourselves, and the Reigersfeldt Chemical factory.

The mock warnings continued causing us to run frequently as far as possible into the woods, but also the bombers came, it seemed, just at about the time the Germans had managed to produce again a trickle of petrol. I was getting tired of the constant vigilance, plus the extra mileage I was covering although there was the advantage of not doing any work through these circumstances. I began to consider that at this late stage, as we all hoped, in the war, the best place to await the oncoming armies, especially the Russians who were the nearest, was at Lamsdorf, Stalag VIIB, and not in a huge oil refinery. I considered the possibility of convincing the German doctor, that I was unfit and so could be returned to Lamsdorf.

As I worked out these details, I naturally consulted my fine friend and partner, Harry Evans. It would mean if I were successful leaving him to face it alone, as indeed would my other two friends, Bert and Len. When I broached this idea to Harry, he was insistent that I should try and achieve a return to Lamsdorf. He agreed it was the most sensible thing to do and considered the chances of survival better at Lamsdorf, where we felt that even the Russians must know of its existence. I was reluctant to consider leaving Harry for I would again be alone and two heads were always better than one in adverse conditions. I remember the argument Harry used as follows.

"Les, it is your duty to your family and yourself to get back to Lamsdorf, if you can. There is not a man here that would not change places with you, if he could".

It was the kind of reasoning I could expect from such a true comrade. Still I decided to consult Bert and Len and put all the reasons before them.

Bert was as firm as Harry, that I should go, and speaking as he always did for Len, not only repeated the same line of reasoning, put forward by Harry, but ended with these prophetic words.

"You can rest assured Leslie, that Len and I will be right behind you, as soon as I have invented suitable complaints with which to see the doctor".

Whether at this stage in the war the Germans realised the end was not far away, or whether the German doctor knew our true purpose was to try and avoid the awful fate of being killed or maimed by our own planes, I do not know. I saw him, and he agreed I should return to Lamsdorf.

Consequently, I said goodbye to Harry, Bert and Len and all those gallant lads at Reigersfeldt. I packed my few possessions, and with another lad who was also being returned, set off with the guard one morning in early November, to march to the railway station. We were allowed to travel in a railway carriage, and on the journey, I was amazed to see for mile after mile, nothing but numerous bomb craters. Now the war was really being brought home to us, right on our doorstep in Eastern Germany.

Evacuation from Lamsdorf - arrival at Moosburg, Bavaria - Self-Promotion

On our arrival at Lamsdorf, we found that there were still thousands of POW's in the camp. They were excitedly and anxiously awaiting their release in due course by the relentless advancing Russian army. Water was severely rationed, turned off most of the day and night. Food was very scarce, half a Red Cross parcel per man, per week, until supplies were exhausted. No one now expected any of the large truck loads of life saving parcels to ever arrive.

There was thick snow everywhere and the weather was very cold. We had virtually no heating and keeping warm was a serious problem.

When my companion and myself had arrived at Lamsdorf, the guard took us into the office run by civilians, which was just outside the camp entrance. We approached a counter where girls were seated busily writing and reviewing cards. One of these, a pretty girl came up to me, and asked my Stalag Number, which was 17063 she turned away, and soon came back with my card with the photograph taken of me in 1940, when I had made an ugly face at the photographer. The guard who was now very docile as they all were, did not interfere, as I asked the girl if I could see the photograph. She handed it to me smiling and I laughed at the awful face I had pulled. So did she, and I said a few words to her and thoroughly enjoyed that brief moment which would have been unheard of even a year ago. I often wondered how these local girls fared when the Russians eventually overran the camp.

In Lamsdorf, nearly every day we saw if the winter sun was shining and certainly heard the heavy American bombers overhead, on their way perhaps heading for Auschwitz or Reigersfeldt.

One day in the sunshine, I saw a huge formation of bombers heading home, watched wistfully by us all. I then saw far behind a lone bomber, obviously in trouble limping along, but how marvelous to see a long range mustang fighter keeping him company, and what a tonic that must have been for the tired, possibly wounded crew. The R.A.F. contingent in their compound would take particular interest in these formations and would shout out advice as to what action to take, especially as we once saw a bomber gradually losing height descending lower and lower unable to keep up. We watched it keenly until it was lost from view, wondering if it ever returned home.

The most wonderful thing occurred just before Christmas 1944. Into my barrack came searching for me, Bert and Len, they had made it back sick. Truly Bert was a wizard. We talked and talked and saw each other every day, a perfect trio, reveling in each other's company. What a pity poor Harry was unable to get back and join us. By December and my last Christmas, a very poor one, in the Third Reich, the lads were claiming it was possible to hear the Russian tanks, the sound borne on the breeze. I think now, although I heard very faintly the grinding of wheeled vehicles and even machine gun fire, it was most probably the Germans.

Slit trenches had been dug in every compound, apparently, long ago. They were now needed for the Russian Air Force fighter planes, were making daily appearances, and strafing the camp it seemed. We all crouched in these trenches and there was no doubt, bullets or heavier calibre ammunition hit the walls of our barracks, but these planes could have been concentrating on the four German watch towers.

There is reason to believe that at this time the Germans were only holding the camp with a skeleton staff, for many had disappeared, whether towards the Eastern Front, or heading West, I do not know. Then came the orders. We were all to be marched out of Lamsdorf, heading West, on that now hopeless and infamous march to nowhere, which settled the fate of many long term POW's. The first to be evacuated were the RAF compound, who were paraded at dusk in late December 1944, clutching their possessions, they hoped to be able to carry. They were marched away at dusk, because of the Russian Air Force planes, that were always about.

The next day Bert and Len called upon me in my barrack and suggested we go into the RAF compound to inspect their vacated quarters. We did so and as we entered we saw neatly arranged beside every 3 tier-bunks, dozens and dozens of suitcases, holdalls, large canvas bags, each with neatly written labels, directing someone to forward those belongings to various parts of the United Kingdom. The three of us roared with laughter at the thought of what the Russian soldiers would do as soon as they entered these barracks. All these cases would be forced open, their contents taken if of any use. It was already happening, as POW's came into the hut and started ripping open bags and taking anything they fancied. We stood aloof watching this scene, we desired nothing extra to carry, being quite sure that trudging through the winter snow, destination unknown, would tax us to the limit of endurance.

Within a day or so, possibly the 30th or 31st December 1944, we were ordered to leave. Fortunately, and we would have arranged it anyway, my contingent contained, Bert and Len. We all formed up at dusk and prepared to leave Lamsdorf. We marched out along the snow covered road to the village. When we reached the main street, a convoy of open lorries, full of very young German soldiers, were seated in these vehicles. Each man was holding a rifle and covered with a white cape from the neck down almost to the top of their Jack-boots. They were going up to the Eastern front and I vividly recall the look in their faces, as they watched us march silently past them. Every face bore the look of a condemned man - Germany was finished and their nightmare was coming true. The feared and hated Russians were almost there.

It was Götterdämmerung![1.]

As we passed through the village and toiled through the snow, we saw dead horses that had been machine gunned by the Russian planes. Not visible were any dead German civilians. All along the road scattered in profusion, were the possessions of the RAF, who had marched ahead some days before.

[1.] *Any cataclysmic downfall or momentous, apocalyptic event, especially of a regime or an institution.*

The large amount of clothing they had individually amassed, including towels, shoes, socks, shirts, uniforms, lay useless, being covered by the falling snow.

I do not know how long this first stage of the march took, but we had covered a few miles and finally reached our first stop, a German farm.

We settled down on straw in barns and outhouses as best we could to await tomorrow. I conferred with Bert and Len, and complained of pains in my legs. I decided not to march any further but to see what happened when I refused. Bert and Len immediately said they would stay with me. Before dawn had arrived, the guards ordered everyone to resume the march westwards, but I noticed about 40 men had stayed put, all complaining of different ailments. The three of us joined them. The few guards were very anxious to be gone, naturally, and were urging all of us to march. We told them we could not go on. The guards solved this problem by selecting one of their reluctant number to remain with us, which he had no option but to do. His face showed his nervous lack of enthusiasm, which we did not share, for we were hoping the Russians would reach us. We stayed on this farm where there was no food available and all we had was the tiny amount of Red Cross food, we had managed to bring along. Somehow, after two or three days of rest, the guard obtained orders from someone at Lamsdorf, to bring us back to the camp.

As we began the march back we were confident the Germans would allow the Russians to release us, especially as there would be few remaining prisoners in the camp. When we reached Lamsdorf, it seemed virtually deserted.

Large sections of the barbed wire was down. There appeared to be no sentries in the watch towers and very few Germans left. Just by the main gate, a party of our lads were attempting the difficult task of digging a rough well in order to obtain water. There were no water supplies now in the camp. We returned to one barrack and settled in. We could now use the remaining empty wooden bunks for fuel, for no one could stop us, so we started little fires in order to melt the snow to obtain water. I was surprised to find just how much snow had to be melted to brew a mug of tea.

We were now eagerly anticipating the Russian soldiers and wondering just how we would be treated. We three were in good spirits.

Disaster struck one night soon after our return. It must have been early January 1945. I was occupying a top bunk and needed to get up in the dark in order to go outside to the latrines. Unfortunately, I slipped and fell heavily on my right foot onto the concrete floor. I managed to walk painfully to the latrines and back to my bunk. In the morning, I saw my right foot was badly swollen. Bert informed the Sgt. Major in charge. As I could not walk, two medical orderlies appeared with a stretcher, on which I clambered. I was taken to the makeshift hospital near the main gate. In the only small room, were half a dozen patients. There were very few medical supplies and no doctors available, as they had all left the camp. A medical orderly put a rough splint on my foot, telling me he hoped it was only a sprained ankle. Bert and Len visited me to cheer me during this misfortune. Another blow occurred, the next day Bert and Len came quickly in to see me, saying they were marching out that evening with the rest of the remaining lads. This was a very sad moment after all we had been through together. I shook hands which them both, wishing them, as they wished me, all the luck in the world. I was never to see them again!

Each day the Russian planes would put in an appearance and an Aussie named Ernie, who had been captured in the First World War, and again incredibly in this one, used to amuse me. As soon as we heard the planes, he would shout out. "Go to it, ground staff. Hit the deck". The medics and helpers would dash outside in to the slit trenches, for we had to remain where we were. Ernie would laugh sarcastically.

After a few days, the medics told us we were all to be moved, by request from the Swiss Red Cross, and we were to be taken in a lorry to Lamsdorf Station, and put in Cattle-trucks, destination unknown.

I was astounded by the news, and did not care for it at all. We had received regular news bulletins, for there had been a hidden radio in Stalag VIIIB. It was common knowledge that the Allied Air Forces, now with no opposition except flak batteries, were hitting everything that moved on the French Railways, and with the advance to the German Frontier, presumably the German Railways. We had no option, anyway we were classified as stretcher cases, although I could and did hobble with the aid of a walking stick on to the German lorry for the ride to Lamsdorf Station.

It was snowing and continued, thus preventing the Russian planes from attacking us. We were placed eight or ten men, as lying down cases in one cattle-truck, quite comfortable considering all my previous travelling experience. The train finally moved off. Our friendly ally the snow, continued off and on, as it was to do during our five day journey to Moosburg POW Camp, not far from Munich in Bavaria, Southern Germany.

As we chugged along, I was determined never to work for the Fatherland again. Although I hoped the war would soon end, it had gone on for nearly five years and might last longer than I expected. I had prepared for this by obtaining from an army uniform the four chevrons, two on each arm to promote myself from Gunner 892705 to Bombardier or Corporal to the uninitiated, Shorrock. I got hold of a needle and cotton from the medics and performed this method of lightning promotion as the train fussed and fumed along. We came to a halt, staying there so long I asked someone to peer through the slit of the woodwork, and try to let us know what they could see. I was informed by our look-out that it was Praha, Prague. This I had to see.

I struggled up and peered through the slit. It was like a fairyland with the snow covering the town, but I clearly remember seeing a castle on the hill, like something from a Walt Disney cartoon. Just at that moment the sun shone through and then I heard the awe-inspiring roar of hundreds of heavies, Flying Fortresses heading our way. As they thundered above us, I prayed they would not bomb the town, as we were locked in, like sitting ducks. They did not, but passed harmlessly, but vengefully onward. It was a very long journey, undertaken in the middle of January 1945. Eventually we came to a halt at a large railway station, according to our look-out. It was a cold evening and

I enquired of our watch-keeper, if he could read anywhere the name of the station.

He replied, "Yes, Munchen. Munich".

I gasped with surprise for this was one of Bomber Commands favourite targets, the home of the Nazi Party, and their famous Beer Cellar.

We stood at Munich for hours and I fervently hoped that our planes would give this town a miss tonight. At last the train pulled out of the station clanking wearily on the way and I am sure we all breathed a sigh of relief. A few miles from Munich the train halted, in the middle of nowhere. Soon we heard the unmistakable sound of the British Lancaster's heading for Munich. The formation passed by, but whilst they were still in progress, we heard and felt the vibrations of the pounding that Munich was receiving. Finally, we again moved off and some hours later we arrived at a railway station, the end of our journey. We got down from our truck, those who could manage, and POW's who could walk were marched away. We were provided with transport in an ancient lorry and off we followed, bound for my second and last POW camp, in the first and last German Reich. It was Moosburg, Bavaria.

Liberation – With the Americans - England at last.
Wolverhampton

Moosburg was a similar but smaller camp than Lamsdorf
Stalag VIIB. It had the usual high barbed wire fence,
inside trip wire and four watch towers, manned by
sentries. I had bargained on the hope that in the confusion
of abandoning Lamsdorf, the Germans would not worry
about our records and even if they did transport them, there
would be an incredible jumble. Therefore, I could safely
assume the unentitled rank of Corporal L.B. Shorrock. I
had chosen this because I looked too young in my own
modest opinion to get away with three stripes, the rank of
Sgt. As I expected, the Germans could not care less, the
war had reached the final stages and we were simply
deposited in a similar barrack block that we had occupied at
Lamsdorf. Any leg cases or foot injuries took over the
bottom bunks.

There were English, American and Russian prisoners at
Moosburg. The Russians of course were always treated
by the Germans as sub-human and had no Geneva
Convention Principles to cover them. I think those at
Moosburg, despite their very hard existence, shortage of
food and no possessions, were probably better off than
other Russian POW's I had seen. They of course were
able to obtain a little food from us, for ½ a Red Cross parcel
per man, was still being issued at Moosburg. The German
food, as at Lamsdorf, was totally insufficient, a little soup
and the now tiny bread ration. The Russians did however

possess in abundance unwelcome guests, bugs, horrible red blooded creatures that gorged on humans. I found it difficult to sleep because of this pestilence and hoped that the lice we had once been so badly and so long plagued with, would not return.

There were wounded American flyers in my barrack, some had limbs amputated. Above me was Chris, an American pilot, who had a bad hand wound and required assistance. I discovered that these flyers, had been part of the group, who bombed the oil refineries, including Riegersfeldt. They laughed when I described the events as seen on the ground by the ungrateful recipients of POW's. I pleased them by telling them of the damage the raids had caused. I brewed them coffee, and looked after them. In return, they related stories supposedly true of all the famous film stars they had seen or met. I had visited a doctor in the camp, who was an American. He examined my foot and thought it was probably only a severe sprain. I carried on walking on it for a week or so longer, then felt compelled to return and again, see him. The doctor was very courteous and told me the Germans had a Fluoroscope, that he would try and borrow. He did this and I put my foot up near a sort of flat screen, being amazed to see the bones of my toes clearly on this device. The doctor apologised, saying I had broken a small bone in my right foot. He then proceeded to put my foot and leg just below the knee into plaster of Paris, leaving my toes free and attaching a walking iron to my foot. I thanked him, knowing I would have to wear this contraption for about six weeks or more. By this time, we were entering March 1945, and all our talk was concerning the end of the war, which now seemed certain from the latest news. General Patton's army was rapidly advancing and wounded officers, with the aid of maps, were marking off each gain and keeping us well informed.

I found it difficult to imagine after almost five years of captivity. I could not get as excited as I knew I ought to be, and yet I wanted to get home as much as any other person.

Perhaps it was the uncertainty of how it would exactly end in our cases that was worrying me. I had experienced Auschwitz, which had changed my whole attitude towards the Germans. Now I knew they were capable of anything, even murdering POW's.

One day, an Army captain who was recovering from a leg wound and walked with a stick, called for our attention. He had with him a little man, with a moustache, dressed in a quaint old-fashioned, worn-out uniform. This person was holding a violin. The Captain addressed us. "I have managed to persuade Mr. So and So, Leader of the Bucharest Philharmonic Orchestra to play for us". The little man bowed, then began to play so beautifully, that we were all transported to another world. The Russians crept in to listen and there was no sound, except the flowing music of an incomparable artist. When he had finished, there was tremendous applause from the audience. The little fellow again bowed, smiling sadly. The British Captain went around seeking cigarettes, which were gladly given and presented them to our superb violinist, who departed with the captain to give, I am sure, another recital elsewhere. I clearly remember thinking to myself, where in the world would another scene like that be enacted.

It looked as if I was going to finish my captivity as I had begun, in a ragged fashion, with one boot on my left leg, a tattered battle-dress uniform, with the right leg cut to enable the plaster cast to be worn. I was also hungry, as of course was everybody else. In the first lovely days of April 1945, I went outside to observe the daily pounding of the nearby German Armies. All around the sky were groups of Allied aircraft bombing on smoke marker bombs. It was a common sight to see several raids in different quarters of the compass, at the same time. If one arose at the first light of day, one could see the returning Lancaster's. The Germans at this stage in the war did not sound air raid warnings anymore. It was just a permanent air raid going on.

Inside the barracks with feverish intensity the military generals were planning our release date. The 27th of April, they announced to us. With all deference to their military genius, I could not really believe that was true, but they were right, or near enough for all that matters. The day of our anticipated liberation dawned and we were up early. I had come a long, long, way, for what now was going to happen. So many lucky escapes or incidents, that I preferred to regard as miracles had occurred. Could they really continue?

Very soon we could hear ominous sounds of small arms fire within the camp. Peering cautiously through the windows, we saw elderly German guards wearing Red Cross armbands, running outside the wire. What had happened was, that these guards who considered themselves only remaining in the camp as caretakers, intended to hand the camp over to the Americans as soon as they appeared. Some SS Units in the woods by the camp, had disagreed with this and were firing on these guards. The Americans soon quietened the SS, then there was silence.

Suddenly a roar of cheering broke out and from our window, which gave a good view of the main road between the compounds, appeared a solid mass of POW's mounted on an American tank which was travelling slowly along. I could not believe that I was liberated, free at last after five long weary years. I felt no excitement, it all seemed unreal.

We waited for hours for some information. Two American Officers from General Patton's Army came around on a quick visit to every barrack, escorted by the S.B.O. Senior British Officer. After that, nothing happened for two days. Fed-up with not knowing, I hobbled out and walked up to the wire fence, where there was a young armed American sentry outside the wire. All around the camp were tanks firing over us. I asked the American soldier for information. He told me the Germans were weakly resisting on a river a mile or so away and they, the Americans were mopping them up. I expressed concern as to whether they had artillery that could shell the camp, as I felt trapped behind the wire. He told me not to worry, there was no danger of that happening. Partly relieved, I returned to my barrack. On the third day, the Americans ordered us to get ready to leave on lorries. In all the confusion since our liberation, we had unfortunately received no food at all, so I, as all the others were very hungry. By the time we had been sorted out, gathered possessions, if any, I had nothing, it was early afternoon before the convoy pulled out.

I well remember sitting in that truck, each of us had taken a blanket, for it was still very cold at the end of April 1945. We made good steady progress in this, the first stage of our journey to freedom. It began to drizzle with rain and as these were open trucks, I put my blanket over my head and shoulders, as did the others. I remember passing fields with dead German soldiers lying in them. We travelled along the banks of the Blue Danube and I saw the water was a dirty green colour, unlike the famous song.

In the late afternoon, we were approaching a village, which I thought would be of no particular interest when I heard a terrific yelling.

"Lofty, Lofty, Lofty".

I looked up and immediately stood up as best I could, and saw in the middle of the road just behind me, a very familiar British POW, which his distinctive mop of red hair. It was Ginger Thomas, a lad from the Karlsthal River Party of 1941. I yelled back to him at the top of my voice.

"Going Home! Going Home!"

As I did so, I was aware of other figures I recognised rushing out into the village street from houses. Now this to me was another miracle, for we had travelled from Eastern Germany to Bavaria by train. They had marched, and the odds of ever meeting up with them at that moment in time seemed absolutely incredible.

At last we reached our destination Regensburg. There was a flying field attached to the Messerschmidt Aeroplane Works. The factory had been completely demolished by raid after raid. There was no cover or shelter, only split and broken timber lying around with lots of mud. We dismounted from the vehicles and were each given a tin of American K. Rations, which had three compartments. I think we had three tins a day, but I cannot be sure on this point. We were told to await transport by planes, which would be flying in, landing on the field to take us home.

I noticed a young tall friendly lad, who was standing near me, and we began a conversation. Like me, he was an old POW and came also from London. His name was Harry. I soon found Harry was a marvelous companion but he was a quiet, thoughtful chap, with a very pleasant manner and we got on famously. I was still hobbling around on my foot iron, in plaster of Paris, and my bare toes were getting wet and cold.

There were quite a lot of POW's standing around waiting. Soon a great shout went up and we saw three or four American C47 twin engine Dakota transport planes beginning to circle our field to land. As they taxied across the grass field then slowly came to a standstill, a surge of POW's rushed madly over to the planes, far too many men for that tiny air fleet. I had started to move and after a few yards my iron on my right foot stuck firmly in the mud. Harry stood by me, as we watched only a few lucky POW's board the planes. The aircraft took off, leaving hundreds behind. I had that feeling that I was again invited to take part in an organised shambles. Perhaps this was unfair in view of the chaos that liberating POW's must have inevitably caused. I told Harry the first thing I must do, is get this wretched plaster off my leg and I thought I knew how.

I had noticed over by the side of the road that led to the village, five Russian POW's, now free, sitting near a homemade fire of pieces of wood. I made my way slowly, with Harry, to where they were sitting. They looked up as we joined them and with a friendly smile together with sign language, I indicated that I desired the removal of my plaster. One of the Russians immediately produced a wicked looking knife and attacked my plaster in a very business like manner, assisted by his associates. It was very hard work, but eventually my plaster in small pieces, plus the leg iron were discarded. Unfortunately, I had nothing to give these people for their inestimable service except another friendly smile and we walked away. I realised that although I was now unencumbered, I had another problem. It was having one worn boot on the left foot and nothing on the right. As I put my right foot down on the cold wet muddy earth, it was very uncomfortable, although I felt no pain, and hopefully assumed the fracture was now repaired.

No further planes had arrived and it looked like a cold night out in the open. I told Harry we must do something to obtain shelter.

At that moment, as if in answer to my thoughts, along the village street towards us came an American ambulance. I immediately put my hand up, as if I were hailing a passing London bus. The ambulance stopped. The American driver and his companion looked me over.

"What's the trouble", he enquired.

I pointed to my foot and started an explanation about the plaster. The American said genially,

"Hop in bud".

His friend got down and took us to the rear of the vehicle. He opened the doors. I hopped in. So did Harry. The American closed the doors, joined his driver, and off we sped. Not very far, for just on the other side of this airfield hidden from view, was an American Field Hospital, comprising tented accommodation.

We stopped at a large marquee and were invited in. There were four or five camp beds occupied by American wounded soldiers, not seriously hurt, two spare beds, one for each of us. My eye was drawn to a vacant camp bed in the middle of the tent on which was heaped dozens and dozens of packets of many brands of American cigarettes. The friendly American soldiers greeted us.

"Hiya fellas". "Where ya from?" "Come right in." Have some cigarette packs."

We thanked them. I took cigarettes. Harry did not smoke. We gave them a brief version of our POW days. They invited us to help ourselves to loot. They had haversacks filled with watches, gold and diamond rings, also bracelets. I looked with wonder at this treasure chest, but decided that if we took any, we would lose it all in a search on our reaching home. How utterly wrong I was. We could have brought anything back with us.

The first call for food made us both eagerly join the G.I's in the queue. The amount of food we received astonished us, for the Americans lived well. We were satisfied as we returned to our tent. In the corner of this large canvas ward, was a very big radio receiver and transmitter, which was operated by an immensely tall Top Sgt. There also appeared an attractive American nurse dressed in uniform, wearing an American helmet. She smiled at us in a friendly way, which we returned. I felt self-conscious of my ragged condition, having only one boot and tattered uniform. I decided to do something about that the next day.

During the night as I was fast asleep, I was awakened by a torch shining on my face. I drowsily saw an American medical man apparently a doctor who appeared elderly. He was wearing glasses. He whispered to me. "Where ya wounded, boy".

I was still unable to pull myself together, so he repeated his question. Wound, wound, I thought in my stupor, so I turned over and showed him my back.

"This is an old wound, son", he said.

"Are you hurt anywhere?"

I merely shook my head and just as I dropped off again, I could hear them waking Harry.

In the morning, this came back to me and I realised they were checking on wounded American soldiers, being brought in. After a wash and a good breakfast, I approached the Top Sgt.

"Do you think you could find me some clothes to wear, Sgt," I asked him. He looked me over, then said.

"Follow me". He took me to another tent, obviously the stores or quartermaster. There I was given a complete American uniform, with a new pair of G.I. boots, with gaiters attached.

I quickly thanked them and hurried back to dress in Uncle Sam's outfit. I was quite pleased at the transformation in my appearance, so was Harry, but his battle-dress was in good condition.

I strutted about the tent obtaining the approval of the American wounded lads. I went outside where two G.I's were standing, watching a few young, aged 16/18 German boys, taken prisoner being escorted by American guards. One lad said to his friend. "Gee, Look at those Krauts".

"Yeah", replied his mate.

"Yeah", I said. They both looked at me. One enquired. "Say, what part of the States you from".

"London", I answered.

"That's in England, how come you are with us?"

I explained as briefly as I could that we were newly released British POW's. The Americans were very interested in our stories. Then one said to me.

"Will you be giving us a hand with the Japs, after you get back?" I decided that having been so well treated, clothed and fed by these people, they deserved a diplomatic answer.

"Well", I said slowly. "That depends on the British Army, when they have checked us over". That seemed to satisfy them.

I felt more confident now of greeting that charming American nurse, since I was once more respectably attired.

That afternoon we were taken to another large tent, where a movie screen was suspended in the middle and soldiers sat each side of the screen. We saw a black and white film, with sound.

This seemed to me a very agreeable place in which to spend a little time. After the film show, I had a word with Harry. "Harry, we seem to have found a nice place here with plenty of food, and entertainment. Are you in a hurry to go home?"

"No Les", replied Harry.

"Good, then let's make the most of it".

Harry was marvelous, he kept close to me all the time. He was the most reliable and true companion one could wish for. I thought to myself how fortunate I had been during my captivity to find these friends.

We were not able to spend long at this hospital, for on 6th May we were told to be prepared to leave. This was quite simple in our case, for all we had to do, was get up and go. To my surprise, a large lorry was backed right up to the tent flap, the tailboard was lowered and after quick goodbyes, we climbed aboard. There were several other POW's on the vehicle, also a Kiwi Flying Officer. The lorry moved off and travelled, I would imagine less than a mile, only to the other side of the airfield, where waiting for us was our own special twin-engined Dakota. As the lorry backed as near to the aircraft as possible, I saw standing by the door, an American army uniformed girl acting as our hostess. I had never been in an aeroplane before, or since, much preferring my feet upon solid ground.

I entered the plane, which had metal bucket seats and found myself flanked on one side by Harry and on my left the KIWI type. I confided to him my misgivings concerning this form of transport, but he told me that there was nothing to it. It was a sunny early spring day, reasonably warm, with blue skies, plus a few small white clouds, that drifted leisurely across. We took off bumping over the grassy field, leaving the ground, in a slow climb, gradually levelling off at about 5,000 feet, according to my aeronautic companion. I was extremely interested, in looking out of the circular windows, to see how clearly and well defined, buildings, rivers, fields, and roads were.

We were flying direct to England, the course taking us over the Siegfried Line also the ill-fated Maginot Line, until at last we left France and crossed the Channel. I can never forget the sight of the English coast on that lovely day. Had I really made it after all. It now seemed like a dream. Our hostess came along frequently talking cheerfully to us, pointing out places of interest and taking the lads, one at a time to the pilot's position to listen to the radio. It was a long flight, 3 ½ hours approximately I understand, then as the evening sun was descending we landed safely at Mildenhall. Ambulances were waiting to take us for a short ride to a very clean army type hut equipped with two-tier bunks. We settled in and were served with tea and sandwiches.

I had selected my bunk, with Harry above and looking forward to the end of an exciting day, when the army, bless them, who never let you down, with their outstanding organising ability, gave the call.

"Everybody out. All out".

We came out, boarded ambulances, then we were driven to a railway station. Waiting there was a train. Where were we going? To Wolverhampton. Harry looked at me with raised eyebrows. I interpreted his look.

"Well you see Harry, it's like this. We have returned home after being prisoners for five years so as we are both Londoners, the Army has wisely decided to send us to Wolverhampton".

We both laughed as we boarded the train, selecting comfortable seats. Those wonderful Red Cross nurses were on the train walking up and down providing us with tea, cakes, pencils, combs, razor blades, and writing paper. The magpie tendency of EX-POW's compelled them to pocket everything offered. The journey was long, some delays must have occurred, but most of us slept whenever we could. We arrived at Wolverhampton, left the train and were sorted out, myself and Harry with three others being taken by ambulance to the Royal Free Hospital, Wolverhampton. We were taken straight up to a long ward, containing wounded soldiers, but also a few empty beds. We settled in, Harry taking the bed on my left. It was now the early hours of May 7th,1945, the day before V.E. day. Victory in Europe.

At about 6.00 am. a very young sister came into the ward to take details and approached my bed. I had been too excited to sleep so was sitting fully dressed in my

American uniform on the bed. The sister began to write down my details and when in answer to her questions, I told her I was British, captured at Dunkirk in 1940, her eyes became wider with surprise.

She looked no more than 20 years of age. When she had completed the form, I spoke to her.

"Sister, I am very hungry, do you think I could get some breakfast?"

"Of course", she replied instantly. "Tell me what sort of food you are able to eat, are you well enough to consume it"? I remember vividly answering.

"I have dreamed of this for years. I would like fried bread, fried eggs, tomatoes, bacon, toast and marmalade, please". She looked thoughtful.

"I think we can manage that, if you are sure you can eat it".

I of course had forgotten all about the severe rationing and such a breakfast in wartime England would be out of the question. "Sister, there is one more thing, I long for, could I have a hot bath, that is the one thing I have missed so much".

That was easily arranged and off I went. On my return, they brought me a beautiful breakfast, but I do hope they did not go short themselves to provide it, for I was completely unthinking in suggesting such a meal.

Later in the day, my foot was X-Rayed and found to be healed then I was also given a medical examination, as were my other comrades.

The nurses in our ward were very young and kind girls, so Harry and I would help them serve the meals, but they would not allow us to wash the dishes for them. They would make us a pot of tea as a reward for joining in the chores. It was announced that the next day, May 8th, 1945, would be V.E. Day and as such widely celebrated, by all those able to take part.

As soon as the medical Sgt. came to see us, I decided to act as spokesman for our little group. Immediately he appeared in the late afternoon asking how we were getting on, I tackled him.

"Sgt, tomorrow is V.E. Day and we would all like to go outside and join in any festivities - how about it".

"Well", replied the NCO. "If you all feel alright, and take care of yourselves, by the way, you will all have to wear hospital "blues".

This was the blue uniform usually worn by wounded soldiers. We readily agreed.

"If we are going out, we must have some money. How much can you let us have?" I asked. The Sgt. was a little surprised and hesitated for a moment before replying.

"I can only allow you five pounds each, but I shall require your signatures, so that it can be deducted from your pay".

That was no problem for us so we all enthusiastically promised to sign. The Sgt. went away, soon returning with five £1 notes for each of us, together with a book in which we scrawled our names as a receipt.

Five pounds was a lot of money in those days, so we were quite contented with this arrangement. Later, the Sgt. took us to a storeroom, where we selected our blue uniforms.

Harry and I were up bright and early on V.E. Day. We breakfasted, donned our blues, *and then* prepared to sally forth into the *joys and wonder* of Wolverhampton. As soon as we had left the hospital behind us, we walked along the streets looking into shop windows. Everyone was smiling and looking so relieved now that the War in Europe had officially ended.

I went into a shop. I think it was Marks and Spencer and saw a pair of black leather shoes, size 11, which would do me nicely.

I approached the girl assistant and asked if I might purchase the shoes, the price of which was £2.10/- or £2.50, half my worldly wealth. She agreed immediately but first I had to produce my clothing coupons. I was brought up with a jolt. Clothing coupons, I had none of those, so I was unable to buy the shoes.

I suggested to Harry that we go into a cafe and have a meal of eggs and chips, bread and butter, with tea. This we did, and certainly enjoyed our first meal outside as free persons. I called the young waitress over for the bill to also give her the usual tip. She told us that everything was on the house that day and would not accept a penny for herself. We thanked her and left. Next, I voted to try a cinema we spotted, so we crossed the road, where I approached the pay desk. I asked for two nice seats and presented a £1 note. The lady cashier waved us inside.

It was all free today, boys. We went inside choosing the best seats, but after about half-an-hour, I was unable to stand the suspense, of not having to pay out any money. We both agreed to leave the cinema and resume our wanderings.

I distinctly recall pulling Harry's leg by saying.

"How can you acknowledge the friendly smiles and pats on the back, from all these people, masquerading as a wounded soldier, while the real heroes are back in the wards".

Harry just grinned with delight. I am sure we spent little, if anything of our respective five pounds that memorable day, but I had a brainwave. I was wondering how I could inform my family as soon as possible that I was home in England, for they had not received any mail from me for some time. I remembered an off-licence about a quarter of a mile from my home, the proprietor of which was related to my aunt. I changed a £1 into coins and finding a public telephone, I obtained the telephone number from the operator via the London directory. I called the off-licence, recognising the voice at the other end. As soon as I gave him my name, he of course remembered me. I asked him if he could get a message to my family, saying I was in England and quite well. He told me to hang on, which I did, for some time, feeding coins into the box.

The next thing I knew I was hearing the excited voice of my elder brother, asking questions. Apparently, the good proprietor had jumped into his delivery van, travelled to my home, broken the news, collected my brother who was available and brought him back. I quickly explained things to my brother and arranged for him to ring me at the hospital in the next day or so.

We returned to the hospital to prepare for a dance the nurses had invited all of us who could stand, to attend. I could not dance, but intended to repay their kindness by joining them. It was a happy end to a very happy day, not quite over, for soon I tumbled into bed, still quite early, for after all we were in a hospital still with casualties. The pretty night nurse sat on my bed giggling and holding my hand, but keeping a careful watch for the sister on her rounds. It was all perfectly innocent fun by two young innocent people on a momentous day after five long weary years.

Home For My 25th Birthday.

Discharge From The Army.

Peace Resumed.

I received a telephone call from my brother informing me that my mother was concerned that I was in hospital and was attempting to arrange a visit. This was out of the question in view of her serious disability; consequently, I decided to discharge myself from the Royal Free, as I felt perfectly well. When I informed Harry, the other lads also, they immediately said they wanted to do the same and go home. We put this to the medical Sgt. who sympathetically understood our natural inclinations. Everything was quickly arranged. We appended our signatures to the requisite document and received travel warrants covering our journey to London. On 14th May 1945, we thanked and kissed our very kind nurses goodbye, and proceeded on our way.

On reaching London, we all parted to go our different ways. Due to the euphoria of the moment, I clean forgot to take Harry's home address, as he in turn did not remember to ask for mine. I thus lost another excellent, staunch companion, whom I have never forgotten and see him today, in my mind, as he then was. I made my way to London Bridge and caught the train for Ladywell Station at 5.55 pm On alighting at my destination, I walked through the churchyard of St. Mary's Church, recalling my boyhood days, which were spent all around this vicinity, with the nearby playing fields of Ladywell Recreation Ground, and Hilly Fields.

I had my kitbag on my shoulder containing my American Army uniform, plus other articles acquired. I had of course been supplied with a British battle-dress uniform. I crossed the main road and was walking along Romborough Way, when out of one of the houses, ran a pretty girl of sixteen years. I vaguely remembered her as a little schoolgirl.

"Are you Leslie Shorrock?" she enquired with a smile.

"Yes, I am", I replied.

"Welcome Home", She said.

I thanked her, thinking that was very kind of her then I turned the corner, there was my home. I entered through the garden gate and knocked at the door. It was a lovely summer evening, the sun slowly descending. I gazed around at all the familiar gardens, with their neat hedges, and summer flowers. The door opened. There stood my eldest sister, now married with a little nephew, I had never seen. I said casually.

"I'm home, Madge".

She burst into tears, as I followed her indoors, where my mother, and all my family were waiting to greet me. One person was missing I found. My great-aunt Helen, who all through the war had sent me her chocolate rations, included in the three monthly personal parcels. My aunt was a spinster and worked as a secretary. She lived in a tiny room, but her one faithful companion was her dog, to which she was devoted. My mother looked after it, as we had a garden, but my aunt came several times a week, bringing the dog pieces of meat, which she saved from her food ration.

She was working late at her office at New Cross on Thursday, preparing the pay packets for the workers, for the next day, when a flying bomb hit the building. She was the only person there. The only one killed. I was extremely sad to learn of this for I was now unable to convey my sincere thanks for her kindness to me. My mother told me, that during the raids in the blitz, when she begged her to stay and use our garden shelter, she refused and walked away home, declaring forcibly.

"I'm not afraid of Hitler".

The next day was my 25th birthday, 15th May 1945. I asked my mother whether she had kept any of the cards and letters I had written her during my captivity. She had, they were in a tin box, which she kept on the table near her. I asked if I might look for one card, and going through them, I found the card I had written as a joke in 1941. In it I had stated.

"I will be home for my twenty fifth birthday". I showed this card to my mother, saying "I told you I would keep my promise".

I was informed by the army that I was entitled to several weeks leave, and I received pay and allowance. I had written to my firm who of course continued to pay my salary, as they had to my mother throughout the war. They had sent to my mother small sums in addition from time to time, so I was extremely grateful to them.

After I had been on leave two or three weeks, I answered a knock on the front door one afternoon. Standing on the doorstep, grinning like a Cheshire cat, was a smart young soldier.

"Yes", I asked him in a friendly manner.

"Who are you".

He stared at me in amazement, and then laughingly remarked. "I've come all the way from East Ham, wasting my precious leave, to find you do not recognise me."

Of course, it was Vic Mason. I was so surprised, and profuse in my apologies. We spent a pleasant afternoon going over old times, before he left. Then I accompanied him to the station to see him off. Vic returned to work on his release in March 1946 and stayed with the company until his job no longer existed. I last saw him in 1960, when I had left the company, which unfortunately went out of business.

To return to June 1945, I went with my brother to collect my accumulated sweet ration, from a local school, which distributed this. I had a large cardboard shoe-box, crammed with bars of milk chocolate. On boarding the tram for the short ride home, the girl "Clippie" conductor, gasped with astonishment, as the lid slipped off, revealing the spoils.

"Is that really all chocolate", she gasped.

"Have a bar", I said promptly.

She took it, and I thought she would fling her arms around my neck at first, but she caught the disapproving glance of my brother, and decided not.

They were happy days, but all too soon I was notified by the Army to report to Billingshurst Depot, in Sussex, where returning ex-POW's, Artillery personnel, were being gathered for rehabilitation. I spent two or three weeks there, where I was examined by army doctors, who decided that I was unfit for further military service. I, together with some other happy rejected lads, were taken into Guildford, to collect our civilian suits, shirts, ties, hat, mackintosh, with which we were issued to enable us to return to everyday life. We also each received 90 clothing coupons, really gold dust in the days of rationing which lasted for some years after the war. Against the advice of my brother, I allowed my sisters to persuade me to give them nearly all these coupons. I later paid the penalty of shabbiness.

On the day I returned from Guildford with my civilian clothing, August 3rd 1945, it was about 6.30 pm a lovely summers evening, with the sun on the decline. I entered the camp, clutching my precious white box under my arm, and decided to visit the mess-tent, in the hope of obtaining a mug of tea. As I entered, I could see at a glance the place was almost empty, except at one table all alone sitting on a form with his back to me in short sleeves, was a fair haired young man I instantly recognised. He had no knowledge that I was there. He was the Anti-tank gunner, I had first seen at Hesdin in 1940 and on at least two occasions on my return to Stalag VIIIB. We had always exchanged a few words. I debated now, how to greet him. I recalled that popular saying of the pre-war cinema days, when trapped in the middle of a row, one wished to leave. Getting to your feet you would say. "Excuse me, this is where I came in".

I walked up to him, and whispered.

"Isn't this where we came in?"

He looked round, smiled happily, got up and we shook hands. He had just come home after all that time, as so many were delayed, especially those picked up by the Russian Forces. I told him how glad I was he had survived. We wished each other the very best of luck, for I was leaving first thing in the morning. I never saw him again.

I applied and received a 20% disability pension of 8/- = 40 pence per week, increased by one shilling = 5 pence in 1947, when I married. I continued to receive this pension until 1949, when I was asked to attend a medical at Gt. Smith Street, W1. On their discovering I had never received any medical treatment, and was quite well, the Army Pensions Department informed me that my pension would be discontinued, but I would receive a gratuity of £40. If I appealed and lost, I would get nothing. Well the pension of 45 pence paid my fares to work for a week in those days. £40 represented some 7 week's pay, so I accepted their offer. I consider I did quite well.

Pat Howlett, my good friend from the Karlsthal working party came and stayed with me for a week in June 1945, and I showed him around the principal places of interest in London.

I returned to work on 15th September 1945, and remained there until 4th September 1959, when the company failed.

I always thought about Harry Evans, of the Reigersfeldt working party, my friend and partner, who I left to return to Lamsdorf in 1944. I still regretted doing so, and often hoped that somehow, he might have survived. One day in 1966, I was coming home from work about 5.30 pm I had left the station just passing some shops and a cafe when I heard a voice calling my name. I turned around to see Harry racing towards me. That was definitely a miracle. We chatted for a long time and I was absolutely delighted that not only had he survived, but his wife had waited five years for his return. Some did, many unfortunately were unable to.

I close my story, firstly paying tribute to all those very gallant men and women of all the services who through their steadfastness and sacrifice enabled us to return.

Secondly, I thank the marvelous Red Cross for gifts on our behalf for keeping us going, looking forward to those lifesaving parcels.

Thirdly, and by no means lastly, to every POW in Germany with whom it was a privilege to share their hardships. Not forgetting our comrades who suffered in Italy, and for those who endured the appalling experience of captivity by the Japanese.

Les Shorrock

15th May 1920 – 21st May 1991

Printed in Great Britain
by Amazon